T0064543

Gentle Birthing

*Creating Gentle
Beginnings Naturally*

Ann Bridges

BALBOA.PRESS

A DIVISION OF HAY HOUSE

Interior Graphics/Art Credit: Ashleen Pearce

Balboa Press books may be ordered through booksellers or by contacting:

Balboa Press
A Division of Hay House
1663 Liberty Drive
Bloomington, IN 47403
www.balboapress.com.au
AU TFN: 1 800 844 925 (Toll Free inside Australia)
AU Local: 0283 107 086 (+61 2 8310 7086 from outside Australia)

Print information available on the last page.

ISBN: 978-1-5043-1464-0 (sc)
ISBN: 978-1-5043-1465-7 (e)

Balboa Press rev. date: 12/02/2020

Contents

Foreword

Birth.

One word, and yet it encompasses so much.

A myriad of feelings, emotions and experiences unearthed and projected all at once.

On one hand, pre-scheduled birthdays, no pain, 'in and out' procedures and the ability to control the process through high levels of intervention seemed like the perfect solution for medical staff and the busy, modern woman — in reality the physical, emotional and spiritual connection inherent in the birthing process suffered, until now.

To ignore the unparalleled power of the mind and the human ability to create "Heaven or Hell" in one's own personal universe is at the very least naïve.

Yet this ability has been, for the most part, ignored for so long in the context of birth and birthing.

The power to create your wonderfully anticipated birthing experience is within you right now. The ability to dream, desire, visualise and intercede on your own behalf is yours and yours alone.

The fact you are reading this book is a beautiful sign you are ready and willing to begin utilising its brilliant teachings — and that is a wonderful beginning.

It's important to be reminded that what and how you focus between now and the birth of your child is indeed the practice that will get you ready for your main event.

Open your mind, learn, implement and repeat. Dutifully practicing what you learn here, right up to and during your big day.

That and your best are the only prerequisites to creating your most blessed experience. Your best will vary from day to day and as long as you focus on doing your best, that will be enough and it will be perfect in exactly how it manifests for the highest good of all concerned.

On this journey, you have embarked on and that begins in its full glory on your birthing day, all you can control is your mindset and willingness to relax and do your best.

Once more, that is all that is required.

Ann Bridges in this wonderful book puts women back in charge of their experience to create their very own empowering birthing experiences.

Use it with the full knowledge that what you learn here and practice brings you safely closer to your most wonderful creation yet — and that in that moment, where you both get to stare into each other's eyes for the very first time, no matter what, everything is perfect in the universe.

Gabriela Rosa

Naturopath, Fertility Expert and Author

Acknowledgments

Thank you to everyone who helped to birth this book! To all the wonderful parents and their babies, it has been wonderful to share your journey with you. Special thanks to my wonderful husband Chris, who has supported me to attend countless courses, helped me with his fabulous technical skills and set up for my birthing classes. Thank you to my patient editor Nicole, my graphic designer extraordinaire and friend Jess, for the stunning book cover. For the graphics inside the book thank you to the big hearted Ashleen. Thank you to the award-winning photographer Rainee for the mesmerising artwork on the cover and the underwater goddess in said photo, Kahlia.

I am eternally grateful to my sister, Gill, who was the first to inspire me with a positive birthing experience; Denise Love, who was my birthing class teacher and later doula trainer, as she empowered me, gave me courage and confidence; my doula Gwen Teasdale who helped by holding the space and believing in me; and also to the positive stranger who briefly spoke to me in the hospital corridor. All these people supported me in realising a different story for myself. And through this book I am going to pass on that life-affirming story to you so that you may have the opportunity to tell yourself a different story and create the best birthing journey for yourself.

Thank you angels for your constant love support and guidance.

Chapter 1:
My story

You are given the gifts of the Gods
You create your reality according to your beliefs
Yours is the creative energy that makes your world
There are no limitations to the self
Except those you believe in.
— Jane Roberts

How does that quote make you think and feel? Maybe you are wondering what it has to do with birthing. I choose that particular quote to assist you to realise, or to remind you, that you are creating your reality and that you can choose to create an amazing birth.

I am assuming that is why you are in possession of this book. You, my friend, are more powerful than most dare to allow themselves to imagine. I am grateful that you are looking at the birth of your baby differently and are willing to recognise how your current thinking is creating your current feelings. Once you see through society's limiting beliefs, fears and anxieties, you come to your innate state of peace and happiness which means you can access your wisdom for birth.

My birthing stories are of empowerment, joy and personal growth through tackling the challenge that is one of life's great rites of passage – childbirth. Through the birth of both of my children and the subsequent work I am now doing, I have had direct experience with the law of attraction in action. I will show you how you can make it work for you too. As one of my ladies said to me when I asked her what she learnt from the birth of her second child: 'I got to see that anything is possible!' What a great piece of experiential education; I can only begin to imagine how that has impacted her life moving forward. This was intensely gratifying to hear as I was fortunate to be present at her second child's birth because she sought my services after having had a difficult first birth. Whether you are a first-time mum or, looking to improve upon your last birthing experience, you can choose your personal recipe.

This is one of my main reasons for sharing my story with you. Through the birth of both of my children I got to see that my thoughts and feelings really do impact and create my reality, that anything is possible, and that the Laws of the Universe are very real and waiting for us to tap into them to create our preferred experience. In this chapter I will give you a brief overview of my birthing journey so you can learn from my mistakes and successes.

During my nurse training (more years back than I care to remember!), I vividly recall my obstetrics rotation. I helped women going through the birthing process in many different ways — epidurals, gas and air, forceps deliveries, caesareans — and this got me thinking that when it comes to my time to birth I want to be well prepared so that I can make the best of it, not leaving it to chance.

As my final essay during my nurse training, I chose the area of "pain" to research and write about. The wimp in me was fascinated by how best to avoid pain! One area that is very well researched and understood in medical circles is the effect anxiety has on the perception and experience of pain. In a nutshell, the greater the anxiety a patient has, the greater the level of pain experienced. From discussions with various women, as well as my personal experience, it was pretty obvious that they are, for the most part, pretty scared at the prospect of giving birth; especially around coping with pain, which is something that can potentially create a self-fulfilling prophecy. Does this ring true for you?

Due to my understanding of how fear and anxiety increase levels of pain, combined with a particular fear of the potential risks of having a needle inserted into my spine (i.e. an epidural), I was motivated to find an alternative to the usual epidural route when I became pregnant myself. I had worked in theatres as an assisting nurse (or scrub nurse, as it is known in theatre) to the obstetricians performing caesareans; I knew that major abdominal surgery was not the easier option. Sure, if I needed one, it was great to have that safety net however, again, the wimp in me was very motivated to look at how best to avoid it. Armed with my insider knowledge of allopathic medicine, and then my subsequent studies on energy healing, the work of Louise Hay and the personal development I had embarked upon through various courses, I knew I could do it — I just wasn't yet clear on how. So I set my intention for as natural a birthing process as possible.

Around this time, I was fortunate to come across a documentary where a woman who, during a cesarean, managed to avoid anesthetic through the use of hypnosis. Here was someone dealing with major abdominal surgery just by using the power of her mind! I was understandably quite blown away by this and it got me thinking; if she could use hypnosis for a surgical birth then using it for a natural birth would be a comparative walk in the park. I then set about looking for a hypnotherapist who could help me in this endeavor.

I also made a choice to go to my local birthing centre, which is a midwife-led service focused on natural birth. As a nurse, I have a healthy fear of doctors! Don't get me wrong, some of my closest friends are doctors. I am aware of the dominant current medicalised and interventionist view of birth. This is a general statement, I know. There are some wonderful, forward-thinking obstetricians in practice and I cover more on this topic in the chapter dedicated to finding your ideal birthing team. Coming from England, where I gained my nursing qualifications and worked in the wonderful National Health Service, paying for an obstetrician seemed to me a costly and unnecessary expense. However in Australia, where I birthed my children, and America, it seems to be the norm to engage the services of an obstetrician; in England you would only see one if you had a problem or if you chose private care.

Another fortuitous and serendipitous event was that I was unable to get into the hospital-run birthing class, so I went to a privately run class by Denise Love (a perfect name for who she is and what she does). Not only did she have a wonderfully calm nature, a positive outlook on birth and a can-do attitude, she also ran a doula school. I knew nothing of doulas before her class. Given my insight into the interventionist nature of the medical model, I realised having a woman who I connected with during my pregnancy and with whom I discussed my preferences and who I knew would be present to support me physically, mentally and emotionally throughout my birthing (as she would not leave for a change in shift), made total sense. This was especially true given I had a wild idea/fear in my head about my husband passing out! (My own dad is squeamish and is known to pass out at the sight of a drop of blood.) I was concerned I could potentially be on my own or worrying about him and not focused on the birth. I didn't have any family in Australia I could ask, so I decided to hire an amazing doula, Gwen Teasdale, and even though Chris, my husband, was a fabulous birthing partner, we were both so glad of her support.

When I began preparing for the birth of my firstborn, Lauren, I focused my thoughts onto what I wanted. I would visualise the room I would have in the birth centre. I couldn't decide between two lovely midwives that I wanted to be present when my daughter was born, so I visualised them both. The day of Lauren's birth arrived and, as I had visualised, I birthed in the very room I had imagined. In addition, of all of the midwives at the birth centre, the two that I had hoped for were on duty together that day and they had to decide who was to catch Lauren. I was blown away!

While I was pregnant with Lauren, I heard some horror stories from well-intentioned friends. I would say to myself: 'That is your story; it doesn't have to be mine.' I needed to be careful to not focus on the potential problems but instead, the miracle that I was a part of. I sought out the stories and experiences that confirmed what I desired for Lauren's birth, instead of getting stuck in thoughts that could take my focus away from my ideal birth. Conversations with my sister were reassuring. Gill had already given birth at that point and she shared with me that she felt that 'birth is amazing'. I also remember during one of my final checkups passing a lady with her newborn, who stopped me to say what a joyous and wonderful experience birth is. These positive stories are the ones we need to hear more of and to see depicted in films and on TV — and they definitely are out there! Remember, you see what you are looking for.

I have come to realise that in my own life that my life works best when I focus on what I do want, despite external events. When I saw the obstetrician at the hospital with my first pregnancy, due to a gestational diabetes diagnosis, I had the opportunity to really test my thoughts and beliefs. It was towards the end of my pregnancy and I had been keeping my blood sugars well controlled with diet. (As a community nurse I had plenty of experience in dealing with, and teaching patients, about diabetes, so I was well aware of what to do to take care of myself.) At this appointment, the obstetrician informed me that I would more than likely have a big baby and if I was overdue, they would have to induce me. He went on to say that this would then, more than likely, cause me to want an epidural. And, due to having a large baby, I might not be able to birth vaginally and would then require a caesarian section (also known as a C-section), so I 'might as well just book it now'.

I couldn't believe what I was hearing! If I had not had my medical knowledge, along with self-belief and determination, I can see how I could have easily acquiesced and booked in for a C-section, assuming that he knew best. He certainly made a lasting impression on me and was even a gift in terms of seeing the importance of being assertive and trusting my intuition and knowledge. I then asked him if I really needed to now go to see the nurse about my blood levels in this visit, as they were stable and had been for quite some time. I had already waited over an hour in outpatients and I knew that I would have to be subjected to another lengthy wait, having experienced this clinic many times before. His response was to wag his finger (maybe he was still a little put out that I had not signed up for his suggested caesarian) and chastise me, 'You are not a nurse here, you are a patient!' So I dutifully waited to see the nurse, who was surprised that I had come to see her, given my medical knowledge and the blood sugar levels I had been recording. What a waste of time, both hers and mine! This experience showed me that on one level, I had asserted what I wanted by not signing up for a caesarian but yet, I had bowed to his point of view, despite the 'charming' way he had treated me! I had steam coming out of my ears when I conveyed my experience to the midwives on my next visit; they knew who he was and his authoritarian style. Fortunately, the following visit to the clinic I saw a different obstetrician who had a teddy bear tie and lived up to his attire!

From my visit to the authoritarian-style obstetrician I realised that, as the poet William Ernest Henley wrote: 'I am the master of my fate, I am the captain of my soul,' I have to take responsibility for my actions despite external pressures. I love the word responsibility, especially when I break it down into two words, 'response' and 'ability', being my ability to respond. I had allowed myself to get frustrated with this man and I'm sure he thought that he was doing the right thing for me from his point of view. I was able to choose how I wanted to respond to his opinion, and I definitely learnt a lot from the experience. My response was to reaffirm exactly what it was that I wanted. I could see that it had shaken me too. As with any challenge in life, it brought a gift. I just needed to take a moment to look for it. I realised that it offered the opportunity to clear any limiting belief that drew this event to me and allowed me to reaffirm to the Universe just what it was that I *did* want, which was to focus on solutions rather than problems.

I ended up going over my due date by ten days and was under pressure to have an induction. This turn of events helped me to realise the power of a 'mind made up'. I had the delightful 'strip and stretch', sometimes also referred to as 'sweeping the membranes'. This was done at the birth centre in the hope of speeding up the beginning of a spontaneous labour. It didn't. The next phase involved the insertion of prostaglandin gel into the vagina, to assist with the softening and dilation of the cervix. This was done on the labour ward and given it takes a few hours, I was allowed to go home. The cervical examination on my return showed that nothing much had happened. I was getting a few contractions so I remained on the labour ward, which was pretty cold given the air conditioning and my attire of a very glamorous, open-backed hospital gown! As you can imagine, I was shivering and rigid with the cold. It was obviously not an ideal environment for relaxation.

At this point, I was keen to go back to the birth centre where I was originally booked, which was down and across a large corridor, so I spoke with the midwife who was looking after me. Fortunately for me, the labour ward was busy and the birth centre was quiet. Knowing how the system works (one of the perks of having been a nurse for over ten years at that point), I knew this would go in my favour. The requirement was that as long as I didn't require a syntocinon drip and I was already in established labour I could transfer to the birth centre. (Syntocinon is an intravenous medication of a synthetic version of oxytocin, also known as Pitocin in the United States.)

As I was not yet in established labour, with erratic contractions which were not lasting very long (45 seconds), my next option was to have my waters broken. Gas and air made this process most amusing! My midwife made a small opening with a hook, which looks like a long-armed crochet hook, and I felt a warm gush of fluid as she punctured the sac. Things really started to move after that, including me! I was able to walk over to the birth centre, stopping for contractions along the way. My determination, and the power of a mind made up, as well as months of hypnosis and creative visualisation had paid off. I got to relax on the double bed in the room I had been visualising. I also noticed a difference in temperature from the cool of the labour ward to the reassuring warmth of the birth centre. Such a simple yet important thing can make a tremendous amount of difference for the birthing mother — it is hard to relax while shivering!

Although my birth experience did not occur exactly as I had visualised, I was able to see that my thought processes had worked perfectly. Whilst I didn't entertain all of the thoughts, images or problems that the authoritarian obstetrician had told me would happen, yet I see now the appointment with him did invite fears to crop up due to the seeds he planted. I was responsible to weed out those thoughts. Can you see what I am getting at? In hindsight with the pressure on me for being overdue, I would have put money on the fact that I was more than likely to have had some kind of medical intervention. I was always very clear though that I would give birth in the birth centre. So all my deliberate and focussed thoughts *did* impact on the outcome.

My personal experience of birth really did prove that I am the writer, director and star of my movie, which is what inspired me to help other mothers to create their own joyful and life-affirming delivery.

Gentle Birthing

I felt amazingly powerful after the birth of my daughter Lauren; I had gotten a glimpse of my true potential to create my own reality. Yes, I experienced challenges along the way, and that only made the victory of birthing my daughter so much the sweeter, because for every obstacle there was a solution or a gift. I came to realise that women are being sold short of this life-affirming rite of passage as they are told only of the horror stories and negative views that the Western world generally holds, and continues to perpetuate, about how the birth experience is destined to be.

I knew that if I can do it, as a definite wimp when it comes to pain, then anyone can do it. The benefits far outweigh the perceived problems and who you are is greater than any obstacle or curveballs that you may encounter. My birth experience inspired me to change careers, to teach and mentor women, and their partners, of their choices, rights and resources to create a natural drug-free birth, if that was what they wanted.

Looking back on the birth of lovely Lauren I could see all the things that I had done and thought that, in turn, had created that birthing experience, including the intention I had set and all the coincidences that had occurred in my reality. It was wonderful and I learnt a lot especially, how to improve on birthing with my next pregnancy.

By the time of my second pregnancy, I had already completed doula training with Denise Love, so when my son was overdue, I felt confident to ask for an ultrasound to ensure everything was well, which it was. I refused the induction offered and went into spontaneous labour the following day. As before, I used creative visualisation and hypnosis. I had also decided to be more generalist about the ideal midwife for the job as I had learnt to allow the Universe leeway by not being too prescriptive (as it has a much better understanding of what is best for me), and she was perfect. These experiences and more have shown me, without a shadow of a doubt, that my thoughts definitely contribute to creating my reality.

I tell all the wonderful couples I have the pleasure to teach, that they are part of the 'positive birth movement' and ask them to pass on their stories of joy, fulfillment and growth in order to turn the tide on the dominant, fearful, interventionist paradigm and create a ripple effect of love and choice.

Chapter 2:
The power of mindset and understanding

'Between stimulus and response there is a space. In that space lies our freedom and power to choose our response. In our response lies our growth and freedom.' — Victor Frankl

I love this quote by Victor Frankl as it highlights every individual's power and ability to respond to external circumstances. In the case of birth, you can have the stimulus of a contraction, and then have a space in which to choose your response. You can respond with fear and anxiety, creating a tense body thus allowing the perception of pain or, you can deepen your breath, relax physically, surrender to the moment and allow the process to build and release with comfort and ease. Your mindset and the understanding that we are all living in the feeling of our thinking moment-to-moment are key.

The power of mindset is all about the thoughts that I choose to buy into and believe, as they will not only impact how I feel in this all-important present moment, they also have a great influence on what I get to experience in my future moments.

In this chapter, we will look at the Universal thoughts, or stories, as I like to call them, that are common for birthing as well as your specific story. There is a process for you to either improve, or completely change, your current story, depending upon your starting point.

I highlight the importance of thought and its effect on creating your experiences, as well as the power of your words, along with your actions.

Again, there is a process that enables you to experiment so that it stops being just theory and starts allowing you to become fully associated with it. This is experiential learning.

The aim of this chapter is to move you into the best mindset, as this is very important in helping you create your ideal birthing experience. With the right mindset and understanding, you are able to see opportunities and anything becomes possible.

Creating your own story

The stories we have been told about birth, and the stories we tell ourselves, can deeply impact us. This is neither good nor bad. The stories can create consequences. If you listen to today's dominant world story around birth, it is one of fear, angst, pain and intervention. Cesarean rates are rising, they are now as high as 30 percent in some hospitals in Australia and over 55 percent in Brazil! Inductions, to 'get birth going', are also rising. (These figures fascinate me, and it feels like the 'which came first?' conundrum of the chicken or the egg: Did birthing become more problematic and require more intervention or did intervention occur and birthing became more problematic?)

Birth in most of the Western World is now seen as a medical event. I love the Monty Python scene, in their film *The Meaning of Life,* where a lady is seen birthing in a hospital surrounded by machines, in particular, the expensive machine that goes PING! John Cleese as the doctor, turns to the mother flat on her back in stirrups and says, 'Don't you worry, we'll soon have you cured!' It gives a wonderful tongue-in-cheek view of the medical model, as many a true word is said in jest. The majority of births now occur in hospitals and, let's face it, hospitals are synonymous with sickness and sick people.

The media also contributes to the current birth story, with its focus on the dramatic, such as in shows like '*One Born Every Minute*', highlighting the medical way of managing birth. The births I have seen as a nurse and doula, as well as my personal experience, wouldn't make very exciting television — there wasn't any drama, very little noise and nothing to see until the end! All that being said, each birth I have had the privilege to attend, including my own, was an experience of joy and wonder, and nothing short of miraculous.

Added to this are the negative birthing stories that many mothers pass on. Most pregnant women have to listen to tales of birthing woe (e.g. 'I was in labour for days!') or contend with looks of pity for her impending birth. Clearly some women do have trauma as a result of a past birth experience, and it is unfortunate that their stories can colour the way that birth is seen by others. Maybe they didn't have the best support and lacked knowledge of how a positive mindset is a powerful tool.

Negative birthing stories can have a huge impact on a personal level and have the potential to alter the narrative we then tell ourselves, so it is important to remember that another person's birthing experience doesn't automatically mean this will be your fate. Don't worry about what others say, do, or have experienced. Just as no two babies are the same, neither are their births.

Remember that the suggestions and statements of others have no power to hurt you unless you buy into them. You have the power to choose how you will react; your understanding of the inside out nature of the world will stand you in good stead. The power lies within you always. You can choose to reject the thoughts and stories of others and affirm how you intend it to be.

Choose your own story as it is what we tell ourselves that really matters. Imagine that you are the writer, director and star of your own movie and you are creating how you would like to experience your ideal birth. Don't buy into the negative stories you have heard, or if you have experienced a less than ideal birth already, avoid limiting yourself by assuming you will repeat the same experience. Allow yourself to dream, to be inspired and to choose what it is that you truly desire. You mustn't be afraid to dream bigger, bolder and more beautifully.

Gentle Birthing

Take some time, grab a notebook and write down what you are telling yourself about birth:

- What are you focusing on?
- Is it tainted by external points of view?
- Is a prior personal birthing experience colouring your story?

Once you have externalised your story, notice if it serves you or not. This is not about judging yourself, just notice what your story is. Come from a place of acceptance; is the story moving you toward or away from what you truly want? Remember there is no good or bad, just consequences. If this story does not serve you or is not to your liking, you can choose to rewrite it now.

While rewriting be kind to yourself; choose magnificent stories and stop permitting the external physical world to dictate your thinking. Trust birth to be joyful. It is an event that will leave an indelible impression on your memory and success depends on where your intention and attention lies.

If you have had a negative birthing experience be careful to keep it in the past, where it belongs. Learn from your mistakes, don't drag them forward with you or stew on them, as this can have the potential to taint your current reality. Keep your story life affirming, which means that the story makes you feel good, and is a celebration of life; it gives you faith that everything will be fine. Then you can see what treasures life will bring.

Tip: Your new story should be written in the present tense. For example (please feel free to add to this and make it your own):

> *I am so happy and grateful now that I am having the most wonderful, easy and natural birth. I have the perfect support team present, and everything flows smoothly. I am calm, relaxed, peaceful and joyous. I feel a deep sense of love during labour and especially as I look into my beautiful baby's eyes.*

Hypnosis can help with this process as it is always best to get yourself into a relaxed state, much like day dreaming. Hypnosis always starts with relaxation, and this relaxed state changes the brainwaves from the normal waking state of beta to alpha. This helps to impress upon your subconscious mind just what it is that you want to think and create, and gives you access to the quantum field, or the infinite field of potentiality. This is an invisible energy force and you can impact on the quantum field and draw from it according to your beliefs and expectations.

Once you become aware of this truth, tap into it. I like to think of it like going to the movies: make sure you flood your mind with thoughts and images that are life-affirming. Spend your time imagining your ideal birth and reread your new birth story often. Enjoy your daydreaming. The action will happen automatically during birth if you have trained your subconscious well before the event, just as top athletes do.

A thought is a substance

'A thought is a substance, producing the thing that is imagined by the thought.'
— Wallace D. Wattles

Everything starts with a thought. The house you call home started with a thought. I thought about writing this book long before I started writing it. I thought about having children before I conceived them, and I have thought about many things before taking the actions needed to bring my thoughts into reality. So when I thought about birthing my respective children, I spent a lot of time thinking about how I wanted it to be.

Because everything first starts as a thought, start thinking now about how you want your birthing experience. Everyone has the capability to go to their personal mind movies, or as Bob Proctor refers to it, 'image-making'. Unfortunately, much of the time people are innocently focusing this ability in the wrong direction! Also experienced or known as worry!

Please be aware of your thoughts and limiting beliefs, as well as those of the people around you. Be aware of other people's fears and limitations knowing you can easily move beyond them.

Who is in charge?

'Doubt is a pain too lonely to know that faith is his twin brother.' — Khalil Gibran

If you say you are going to do something, do you do it? Do you keep your word? Do you make it important? If you answered yes to these questions, then you are on the right track to create magic in your life. If not, read on to get going on this track.

It sounds so simple to keep your word and yet I know how, in the past, I sometimes let things slide, not realising the consequences of my actions. Sure, on the whole, I thought of myself as reliable, yet there were times when I let myself down, unintentionally or inadvertently.

Now however, I am a lot more careful about what I commit to, whereas in the past I might have said yes to everything and then felt guilty for not following through. Let's face it. We've all done it to a greater or lesser degree, unless you are heading for canonisation! Not to judge, as it is neither good nor bad. We just need to recognise that it has consequences. One of which is the possibility of lowering your vibration due to thoughts of guilt and shame. This can then create a cycle of negativity which does not serve you and you end up going down the path of worry.

The reason I have discovered why it is so important to honor my word is because if I keep breaking my word to myself, I no longer believe or trust what I say and that has consequences.

The first agreement in Don Miguel Ruiz' book, *The Four Agreements*, is to be impeccable with your word: "Your word is the power that you have to create."

With hindsight, I could see I was using the power of words against myself, letting myself down and then berating myself. I uncovered that I was letting my disgruntled self-defeating side win out, and the more I let it win, the more of a victim I became. I was no longer in charge.

The Cherokee legend of the two wolves is pertinent here:

There was a wise old Apache Indian, who was talking with his grandson one afternoon, and he told him that inside of him, and indeed everyone, there is a battle raging between two wolves. One is the wolf of anger, hate, frustration, fear, jealousy and greed; the other wolf is the wolf of love, harmony, cooperation, joy and peace.

To which his grandson asked a very bright question: 'Grandfather, which wolf will win?'

The grandfather smiled knowingly and replied 'the one that you feed!'

When you make an agreement, you experience the battle of the two wolves. By honoring your agreement with yourself, you ignore the wolf of anger, hate, frustration, fear, jealousy and greed and feed the wolf of love, harmony, cooperation, joy and peace, taking charge of your life. This results in creating magic, synchronicities occur and your dreams start to become your reality, often even better than you could have possibly imagined. This, in turn, can stop the potential life-sucking result of being a victim of circumstance. The wolves, depending on which one you feed, can moan words such as 'I haven't got enough time now', 'I'm tired', 'I've been working so hard', 'take a break', 'it doesn't matter anyway', or it can say things like: 'I can do it', 'it is possible', 'I am going to feel so good completing this', 'remember to have fun with this' and on it goes too. You may need to quiet your busy mind in order to feed, and hear, the wolf of love, harmony, cooperation, joy and peace. This is your higher self, your intuition, or your wisdom, which is who you really are. It will give you insights into playing the game of life that are specific to you and your current situation.

If you have not been honoring your word, have some fun and play this little game. Make a daily agreement for ten days. Keep it small to begin with if you are not used to flexing this muscle. Often the ego wants to go for something big and impressive, like swim 10 kilometers every day. Instead, make it practical, something that is life-affirming for you personally.

Examples include flossing your teeth every day; give a compliment to someone, or to yourself; write three things you are grateful for each day or tell your partner you love them; send love to your beautiful baby developing inside of you; practice your birthing affirmations or read your ideal birth story that you have written. Choose something that will enhance your world, and let the fun begin!

The more I have played this game, the bigger the agreements I have taken on, and the deeper my feeling of trust in myself has grown. My world has expanded as I have pushed through the now clichéd comfort zones. This approach stood me in perfect stead when it came time to birth because I knew that I was in charge of how I responded to events. Some responses were better than others, I will admit! And, I trusted that I could get on with the business of birth; I had made up my mind. I have discovered after all, that life is best when lived from the "go for it" perspective! I have found the Universe to be kind, and when I take on challenges, I am supported.

Trust is an important part of birthing and life generally. Where do you stand with trust? Do you spend your time in worry and fear, thinking that the world is a dangerous place and that you need to be vigilant at every turn? Or do you trust that everything will work out? Do you believe that the Universe is a benevolent place and that life supports you?

Don't just hope things will work out for, at that level of commitment you are not playing your best game and your results will suffer as a consequence. Take charge: this is your birth! Dare to play a bigger game, test your mettle. Let's face it, life is a contact sport!

In summary:

- We all have the power to change the collective story of birth, one birth at a time.
- Be aware of the power of your thoughts and the story you create.
- Create your ideal birth story, relax and think about it often.
- Feed the good wolf.
- Trust yourself by proving you can keep an agreement and reap the rewards.

Chapter 3:
How to get your subconscious to work for you

"There is a thinking stuff from which all things are made, and which, in its original state, permeates, penetrates, and fills the interspaces of the Universe." — Wallace D. Wattles

To a large extent your habitual thinking and imagery moulds and creates your reality. One of the master secrets of the world is the marvelous, miracle-working power found in your subconscious mind. This is the last place most people would look for it, which is the reason so few ever find it!

The first thing to understand is that your subconscious mind is always working, it is active night and day and is the builder of your body. You cannot always consciously hear or perceive its silent inner process and yet, it is always expressing, reproducing and manifesting, according to your thinking.

Sometimes there is a part of us (the ego) that seems to enjoy the negative, gossiping about some poor unfortunate or berating ourselves for not being better, more clever, prettier, richer... and on and on it can go. Does this sound familiar? Even our news is geared up to tell us of all the disasters, terrible people and problems of the world. Good news doesn't seem to sell.

Most of us are brought up on this diet of fear and worry, so it is not surprising that it is the normal way to think for most people.

For this reason, your job lies with your conscious mind. Keeping your conscious mind busy with the expectation of the best is important so habitually think grateful, harmonious, joyful, pleasant thoughts. Be aware: you can take charge of the direction of your thoughts. No one can choose your train of thought for you so start noticing them, particularly the thoughts that take you away from your happiness and peace of mind.

If you are feeling anxious or upset it is because you are experiencing some upset or anxious thinking at some level. Your emotions are your Satellite Navigator; access them for guidance. It's like driving across a rumble strip on the side of the road, it wakes you up to where you are heading. All you need to do is steer the wheel to bring you back on the road toward peace of mind. You will then feel a shift in your emotions letting you know you are back on course.

Just as the water takes the shape of the pipe that it flows through, your life principle flows through you and manifests according to your thoughts. Think of it as a living intelligence, Prana, Chi, or even, The Force, as they called it in Star Wars! Know that the life principle is continually flowing through you, so impress upon it the image you desire. Have fun with this process. Remember you are the writer, director and star in your movie, so let's avoid the horror stories and focus on the love story of your baby's birth. In this chapter, I show you how.

The beauty of birth

Suffering may be our interpretation of stimulus, and birth as a stimulus has had a pretty bad rap over the last few decades. What if it doesn't have to be that way? What if you could change your mind from one of fear and anxiety to love and excitement? Do you think it is possible to experience joy and personal growth through giving birth?

My personal experience of birth did just that. It is what inspired me to help other mothers to create their own joyful, life-affirming delivery. I felt amazingly powerful after the birth of my daughter Lauren; I got a glimpse of my true nature to be a participant in creating my reality. Yes, I experienced challenges along the way, and that only made the victory of vaginal birth so much the sweeter. With my own experiences I discovered a solution for every obstacle. I came to realise that women are being sold short on this life-affirming rite of passage. They are stuck in the horror stories and negative view that the Western world generally holds, and continues to perpetuate, about how the birth experience is destined to be.

My experiences – being a definite wimp when it comes to pain – assured me that with the right mindset and understanding, other women can also stack the odds in their favour to create the birth experience they desire. The benefits far outweigh the perceived problems and who you are is greater than any obstacles and possible curveballs that you may encounter. This was where my passion was born to help other women design their ideal birth experience. It inspired me to change careers, so that I could teach and mentor women and their partners and make available the resources that I knew could help them.

I understand that today's women have lots of birth options and it is great that so many advances have been made in medicine. That being said, it seems to be quite tricky in Australia, at the time of writing this book, to have a home birth even while some other countries currently promote home birth whenever risk is absent.

As pain is a subjective experience, personal to each individual, and after sharing all the information and options, if a mum chooses an epidural, I respect her decision. I just want to ensure that it is an informed choice and not one made out of fear. Remember that fear and anxiety make things worse in any situation.

There is a current view of birth that it is difficult, painful and potentially fraught with danger. It is no wonder that so many women are scared at the prospect of birthing and may entertain the options to take the drugs available to get them through it.

Tapping into our energy

Although we as humans and our Universe look solid, we are in fact energy vibrating. Albert Einstein defined matter as a form of energy. The molecules, which make up everything, consist of atoms in a permanent state of flux. From this, we now understand that everything is vibrating.

David R. Hawkins, in his book *Power versus Force,* talks about the fact that everything in the Universe gives off an energy pattern of a specific frequency. For instance, Hawkins assigns courage a frequency of 200 MHz. This is within the calibration of 1 to 1000 MHz. There are no good or bad energies, just frequencies from low to high. Simply stated, powerful attractor patterns strengthen us while weak patterns deplete us. This is why it is so important to be mindful of your thoughts and words as they can, and do, physically impact you.

It is essential that you realise that you are more than capable of birthing with ease and in a state of calm. One of my clients, Agnes, was amazed to find that when she went to her routine checkup on her official due date, she was already four centimetres dilated. She had spent the day going to the hairdresser, shopping and out for lunch as everything felt normal. In addition, her baby was in a posterior position, which is where the baby's spine is situated next to the mother's spine and is often expected to cause the mother increased discomfort.

In his book, Hawkins explains we can strengthen our bodies via high-power energy attractor patterns, which releases endorphins and provides a tonic effect on all of the body's organs. The opposite effect with the low-power energy attractor patterns, is the release of adrenaline, which suppresses the immune system and creates the fight or flight response.

Note: I want to impress upon you the innocence of our thinking. Nobody wakes up in the morning thinking, "I am going to scare myself with my thinking." Yet, this is what we sometimes fall into and it is important not to have guilt or regret about lower frequency thoughts, as this just serves to again keep your vibration at lower levels. They are an opportunity just to notice and choose differently.

The power of thought

A lot of what we think is a result of ingrained patterns, so it can take some practice to change our habitual thinking. To start, just notice your thoughts without judgment and then aim to change them if they are not serving you. Also, remember that an external event does not cause stress but it is the way *you think* about that external event that does – your internal world shapes your external experience.

When Agnes was told that her baby was in a posterior position, as opposed to anterior (where the baby's spine is facing outwards), she chose to talk to her baby reassuringly and held the belief that he would turn at the perfect time for birth and would be a happy, easy baby. All of which occurred!

The human body also has energy that flows in and through it. Different cultures adopt the concepts of energy and its guidance. In Indian yogic tradition these channels are known as 'chakras' through which 'prana', the universal energy, flows. In Chinese medicine there are 'meridians', through which 'chi' or 'qi' flows. This is the universal life force that permeates all living matter.

Energy is everywhere. In its subtle form it exists as spirit and, in its more dense form, as animals, plants, minerals and, of course, us. Sages have been saying through the years that every particle of matter in the Universe is made up of energy. Science is finally catching up and now proving that to be true. Likewise, David Bohm, an American theoretical physicist, contributed ideas to neuropsychology and the philosophy of mind including that there is both a visible and an invisible Universe; again, something the sages have been saying forever. You, my friend, are a spiritual being having a human experience.

The chakras

What are *chakras*? The concept of chakra features in both tantric and yogic traditions of Hinduism and Buddhism. The word is derived from the ancient language of Sanskrit and translates as 'wheel of light'. In this human energy system, the body is surrounded by an energy known as the 'aura'. The aura is made up of seven layers of subtle energy, with the layer closest to the body being the 'etheric body' and it is here that the energy of the chakras exists.

According to shakta theory, which has become popular in the West, there are seven chakras, or energy centres, within the body, and each has a certain frequency that correlates to its colour. These correspond to the colour sequence of the rainbow, in colours and order. Each chakra also stimulates a particular gland in the body's endocrine system. The endocrine system governs our hormones, which regulate our metabolism, growth, development, mood and birthing.

- The **Root or Base Chakra** (red) sits at the base of the spine and is the slowest vibrational frequency. It stimulates the adrenal glands and the kidneys. It is the most primal energy we bring to life. It also reflects the collective attitudes of our culture, family and ancestry. The emotional issues it represents are structure, stability, security, patience, order and manifestation.
- The **Sacral Chakra** (orange) is located around two inches below your navel and nourishes the reproductive glands, ovaries in women or testes in men. It represents the emotions of wellbeing, sexuality, abundance and pleasure. This is often the most dysfunctional chakra in modern culture.
- The **Solar Plexus Chakra** (yellow) sits directly under the diaphragm, in the region of the stomach, and feeds energy to the pancreas. The emotional issues governed here are self-worth, confidence, choice and power. This chakra is strengthened by honouring ourselves and the choices we make. It is important during the birthing process that you do not give your power away and that you take responsibility for making your choices.
- The **Heart Chakra** (green) covers the chest and upper back and stimulates the thymus gland. It is the centre of the energetic body, as well as the central theme of life. Not surprisingly, the emotional issues are love, harmony, peace and unity.
- The **Throat Chakra** (blue) is located in the throat and the back of the neck, and it nourishes the thyroid gland, which strengthens the immune system. Naturally the throat chakra represents communication, truthfulness, creativity and willpower. This delicate centre can be thrown off balance when we do not express our feelings and submerge our ideas. To strengthen this centre, it is essential to know that what you have to say is important and makes a contribution to the whole.

- The ***Third Eye or Brow Chakra*** (indigo) feeds the pituitary gland, which is very important during the birthing process for the hormones it secretes support birthing. It is located between the eyebrows. Emotionally it governs imagination, intuition, knowledge, discernment and wisdom. Blockages in this area can create a sense of confusion about what is real and loss of faith in your connection to the Universe. Regular meditation can strengthen this area.

- The ***Crown Chakra*** (violet) sits at the very top of the head and stimulates the pineal gland. It gives us inspiration, allowing us to see the beauty in all things and healing. The crown is our channel to the divine, our higher self or the eternal realm of the soul or whatever you perceive that to be. Being open to our own divinity and the Source are ways to strengthen this chakra.

Figure 3.1: The location of the chakras in the body

Soul Star Chakra	white	Connection with the Divine
Crown Chakra	violet	Spirituality
Third Eye Chakra	indigo	Awareness
Throat Chakra	blue	Communication
Heart Chakra	green	Love, Healing
Solar Plexus Chakra	yellow	Wisdom, Power
Sacral Chakra	orange	Sexuality, Creativity
Root Chakra	red	Basic Trust
Earth Star Chakra	brown	Grounding

As well as the seven chakras that flow through the body and its structures, there are two other chakras in the etheric body:

- The first is the **Earth Star Chakra** *(brown or black)* which is located 30 to 45 centimetres below the soles of your feet. It connects you to mother earth, Gaia, and keeps you grounded and protected. It is ideally used to ground you and discharge into the earth excess energy or negativity and draw up the energy and vibration of Gaia.
- The second chakra is the **Soul Star Chakra** (white), situated around a hand width above your head. It is the point where spiritual energy enters and flows into the body from the crown chakra. For that reason, it is sometimes known as 'the seat of the soul'. This chakra is involved with the emotion of letting go and allowing the Divine to fill your life.

Chakra balancing methods for birth

There is a wonderful technique for aligning your chakras and getting them back into balance. It can help teach you how to allow energy to flow, raise your vibration and get you connected to your intuition – or higher self, wisdom, divinity, etc. It is a process that I was inspired to create called **'Chakra balancing for you and your baby'**. This technique is based on a process detailed by Alma Daniel, Timothy Wylie and Andrew Ramer in their book, *Ask Your Angels*.

For this you will need to create a time when you will not be disturbed. You can light a candle and surround yourself with your favourite crystals, if so inspired. It will still work either way; the intention is the key as in all things. Read through the instructions ahead of doing the process so that you can focus on the experience, or you may like to record yourself on a digital device. Just remember to read it slowly so that you can have time to experience each stage. I have created a MP3 of this process, which you can download from my website at www.gentlebirthing.com.au.

First get yourself comfortable and close your eyes if you wish.

Imagine you are in a beautiful place in nature that you love, either from somewhere you have been or maybe even somewhere you would like to go. You choose.

Now focus on your breathing, breathe deeply and fully, engaging your diaphragm as well as breathing with your chest.

Notice if you are holding any tension in your body and, with every exhalation, breathe the tension away. That's right.

Just imagine a wave of relaxation floating down through your body, releasing and relaxing any tension as it goes.

As you relax, picture roots growing down from your root chakra, and the soles of your feet, through your Earth Star Chakra and deep down into the earth, to Gaia's very core. Once there, discharge any fears, worries or concerns that you may have right now, down into the earth and allow mother earth to take these fears and transmute them.

Imagine now that you can breathe through your roots and breathe in the energy of the Earth. Bring this energy up through your Earth Star Chakra into your body at the Root Chakra, cleansing and clearing as it moves through each chakra in turn. See the colours of each chakra as the energy moves up. Brown at the Earth Star, flowing into red at the Base Chakra, orange at the Sacral, yellow at the Solar Plexus and green at the Heart Chakra. Imagine each chakra spinning with the beautiful light of its vibrational colour.

Like a fountain, the energy from the Earth continues to rise up now, to your Throat Chakra and use the energy to cleanse and clear to reveal the spinning blue wheel of light.

Next draw the energy up to the middle of your forehead, which is your Third Eye Chakra and perceive the indigo colour of this chakra that allows you to expand your awareness.

Allow the energy to continue up through the violet Crown Chakra and beyond to the Soul Star Chakra, where the energy that has been building, then cascades back down over your body and your baby's body like a fountain of light, cleansing, clearing, harmonizing and balancing all of your chakras.

Keep breathing deeply as you sense all of your chakras spinning vibrantly. Then, when you are ready to imagine tendrils, like branches shooting from the top of your head up and through your Soul Star Chakra out into the cosmos, connecting with the heavenly bodies of the moon and stars. Now imagine energy, like a waterfall, flowing down through yours and your baby's body. Again allow each chakra to glow and be filled with the light flowing down and back into the Earth through your Earth Star Chakra, so that Gaia too, may glow more brightly.

The energies of Heaven and Earth are now flowing through you and your baby; you are grounded and connected to Heaven and Earth. Feel yourself as a living rainbow of light!

Breathe into the bliss of this, and when you are ready become aware of your body and in your ideal time comfortably open your eyes.

Notice how you feel after this exercise. You may like to note down any inspirations or insights you may have had. Also, be aware of how the world looks after the process. I always notice things look brighter and more vivid afterwards. If, during this meditation, you feel more activity from your baby, it may be due to creating more space for them as you relax, as well as them enjoying the energy flow.

Don't worry if you lose concentration or focus, it can take practice. Just note where you lost focus, as this may be an indication of an area that may require further work for you and remember, the more often you practice this, the easier it will become. Some of us are more visual than others. During this process you may not get a crystal clear picture and that's fine. If I were to ask you to tell me the colour of your front door for instance, you would picture it in your mind's eye, it may not be a very clear picture. That is normal for some of us.

Another way to balance your chakras is to have someone else balance them for you. As a Reiki teacher, energy healer and Angel Intuitive, I have had the pleasure of seeing the difference people feel after a session. Often I am able to pick up messages in the form of songs. During one particularly memorable session with an expectant mother, a song kept popping into my mind. Once we were complete with the balancing and energy healing, I asked her about the song. It turns out that was the song they had chosen for their upcoming wedding dance.

We all have different senses that we can use; the visual aspect is just one part. We experience our world with all of our senses, as well as our own personal insights. So go with what arises as this is perfect for you. No pressure! This process should be fun!

Taking the time to just 'be'

Acupuncture is another way you can get your energy flowing. Let's face it, we could all do with a pick-me-up from time to time in order to deal with this fast-paced world that we live in! With so much time spent 'doing', it can be transformative to allow yourself to just *be*. So make time to just *be*. No matter whether this is your first, second, third or even fourth child, carve out some time to balance your energies, either through the process above or with the help of a practitioner.

Another benefit of doing your own chakra balancing is that you are grounding yourself. When you come to birthing, it is all about opening up, to be able to open up and remain grounded will serve you well. Practice makes perfect! You can use this process any time during your labour, as well as during pregnancy, to give you energy, strength, relaxation and calm.

You can also call on your angels for help and guidance. Remember they are respectful of your free will, so you must ask for their help. Mother Mary, Queen of Angels, is someone you can call upon during the birthing process. She helped to give me the strength in order to cope with the intense parts of the labour of my first born. Archangel Michael is there to help you with courage and strength. Angel Jophiel will help you release negative thoughts and Gabriel helps with babies. These are all part of the bigger picture that is waiting for you to call upon them.

If you knew who walks beside you on the way that you have chosen, fear would be impossible. – A Course in Miracles

In summary:

- You are a spiritual being having a human experience. You *have* a body, but you are not *just* your body. Use the support of the heavens as it can make your life so much easier in many ways.
- Angels can fly because they take things lightly! Trust and know that they can help.
- "Let go and let God" has been one of the most liberating and yet one of the scariest things for me to do. It helps in the process of manifesting your dreams.

Chapter 4:
Nutrition — supporting your body and baby during pregnancy

'Let food be thy medicine and medicine thy food.'
— Hippocrates

Pregnancy is a great motivator to overhaul your diet with a positive focus and drop any bad habits, as this will give both you and your baby the optimum nutrients and energy for growth and development.

Some mothers experience nausea in the first trimester, which can be debilitating and certainly no fun! This may feel worse on an empty stomach, so it is best to eat little and often and keep it dry and bland. Simple foods like crackers, which you can carry easily with you in case of emergency or toast, wholemeal or wholegrain, when you have access to a toaster. Ginger is one of nature's remedies for nausea; slice a bit of ginger root and allow it to steep in almost boiling water for a beverage, or consider pickled ginger or ginger tea.

It is important that you focus on nutrient-rich foods, rather than the empty, sugary junk or fatty snacks. For example: ice cream or hot chips. Before you demolish that chocolate cake, remember that you are not eating for two! In fact, in the first trimester, you don't require any increase in food intake. By the second trimester, an increase of 1400 kilojoules is recommended and by the third trimester, 1900 kilojoules.Remember that an apple is around 300 kilojoules and a serving of brown rice (1 cup) is 904 kilojoules. (1 calorie equals 4.184 kilojoules.)

To give your body and your baby the best nutrition in order to flourish during your pregnancy, include the following essential vitamins and minerals. Where possible, buy organic foods to reduce your potential intake of pesticides. Regardless of whether or not you have access to organic food, be sure to wash all fruit and vegetables thoroughly.

Essential minerals

Calcium

Calcium is essential for the growth of your baby's bones, teeth, as well as the muscles of the heart and nerve development.

Sources: Most people turn to dairy products as a good source of calcium; there are plenty of alternatives to dairy if you are lactose intolerant.

- Broccoli is a great source of calcium along with other dark green leafy vegetables such as kale and spinach.
- Calcium is also found in many beans.
- Oranges, as well as having calcium, contain vitamin C (as does broccoli) which aids the body with the absorption of calcium.
- Quinoa is a delicious, healthy whole grain that contains calcium. Sesame seeds and chia seeds are another good source.

Folate

Folate is required for your baby's neural tube development, in order to prevent spina bifida and other defects of the spine, brain or spinal cord. Folate is often shown as one and the same with folic acid. Folate is the natural form of vitamin B9 found in a variety of foods, while folic acid is the synthetic form of the vitamin, and is often found in supplements and fortified foods, such as cereals. Both are readily utilised by the body. The advantage with the naturally occurring folate is that the body is more able to regulate healthy levels excreting excess through the urine.

Sources: There is a wide range of delicious foods to choose from that will ensure you are getting all the folate you need.

- Dark leafy vegetables such as kale, spinach, romaine lettuce, broccoli, and asparagus. Asparagus is one of the most nutrient dense foods with just one cup of steamed asparagus accounting for nearly 65 percent of your daily folate needs.
- Lentils: One cup provides 358 mcg of folate, which is 90 percent of your daily requirements.
- Beans: Pinto beans boast the highest folate content; one cup will give you 74 percent of your daily needs.
- Avocados: One cup can cover 22 percent of your requirements for the day.
- Fruit: Citrus fruits rank the highest.
- Seeds and nuts.

Iodine

An essential trace mineral, iodine is used by your thyroid to produce hormones that are needed for the development of the foetal brain and nervous system. During pregnancy and breastfeeding your iodine requirement increases from 150 mcg to 290 mcg daily.

Sources:

- Organic strawberries can give you up to 10 percent of your daily iodine needs in just a single serving.
- Beans: Organic navy beans are top of the list of beans for containing iodine; many other beans are a great source too as well as providing much-needed fibre.
- Organic yogurt: 1 cup contains around 90 mcg.
- Cranberries: As well as being a wonderful antioxidant, they are great for preventing urinary tract infections and will also top up your iodine intake. (Be mindful certain brands of store bought cranberry juice may have a high added sugar content.)
- Potato: One medium baked potato holds 60 mcg of iodine. Additionally, leaving the skin on provides extra nutrition.
- Sea kelp: Perfect source to get the highest amount of iodine into your diet - one tablespoon can give you 2000 mcg!

- Kombu, an edible kelp: A piece one inch in size will give you approximately 1450 mcg.
- Himalayan salt: One gram contains 500 mcg, and it isn't chemically processed and stripped of natural health properties like many other enriched table salts.

Iron

The blood volume in pregnancy increases, on average, 45%, but can actually be up to 100%. There is also increased tissue growth during this period. Iron is needed to make the healthy oxygen carrying red blood cells during this time of volume increase - throughout the pregnancy, starting in the first trimester.

Iron is transferred to the placenta, at the expense of the mother, in order to support the foetal development which can cause fatigue, weakness, shortness of breath and overall discomfort. Ideally there would be adequate iron stores at the beginning of the pregnancy however supplementation has shown to increase irons stores in both the mother and the newborn baby.

There are vegetarian iron tonics, which are pleasant to taste and can top up the iron levels that commonly drop during pregnancy. (Floradix is a vegetarian product for iron.)

Sources:

- Meat, beans, eggs and tofu are all iron-rich proteins.
- Dark green leafy vegetables like kale and spinach are great, and also have the added benefit of containing vitamin C, which is required for the absorption of iron by your body.

Omega-3

Omega-3 is an essential fatty acid that plays an important role in your baby's brain function and nerve development, as well as being important for the formation of every cell in the body!

Sources:

- Oily fish (e.g. salmon, trout, mackerel and sardines)
- Pumpkin seeds, brazil nuts, flaxseeds and flaxseed oil, walnuts.
- Spirulina.

Zinc

Zinc is particularly important during pregnancy and breastfeeding as it aids cell growth due to its role in protein building. It also supports your immune system.

Sources:

- Pumpkin seeds, wheat germ, Brazil nuts, chickpeas (hummus is a great dip), and sesame seeds.
- Garlic.
- Dark chocolate – my personal favourite, Lindt chocolate 78%! Go for good quality chocolate which is high in cocoa. It's rich so a little goes a long way.
- Legumes, beans and nuts as well as whole grain products and fortified cereals.
- Red meat and chicken.
- Dairy products.

Essential vitamins

Vitamin A

Also known as beta-carotene, vitamin A is crucial for immune system health. It also plays a very important role in the maintenance and health of an assortment of bodily systems, from bones and skin, to the copying of genetic codes between cells. Your baby depends on it for the development and growth of their tissues, cells, vision and their immune system too. Severe vitamin A deficiency has been connected to vision loss in children in third world countries. On average, a healthy daily intake of vitamin A for pregnant women is approximately 4000 IUs.

Too much vitamin A can potentially cause an increased risk of birth defects, so it is best to avoid foods very high in the retinol form of vitamin A during pregnancy, such as liver. Avoid prenatal vitamins that contain any of the retinol forms of vitamin A; look for beta-carotene instead.

Sources:

- Fruits and vegetables, particularly those that are orange and yellow, such as carrots, oranges and lemons.
- Leafy green vegetables are a good natural source.
- Some cereals and milk are fortified with vitamin A.

Vitamin B12

Vitamin B12 is needed to activate folate in your body. Not having enough in your diet can increase the risk of your baby developing a neural defect (see folate). Vitamin B12 is also required for proper blood cell formation, neurological function, as well as DNA function.

Sources:

- It is naturally found in animal products, fish, poultry, meat, eggs, milk and milk products.
- It can also be sourced from fortified cereals.
- Vegans will need to take supplements or use fortified foods to ensure an adequate intake.

Vitamin B6

Vitamin B6 helps your body to metabolize protein, fats and carbohydrates. It also helps to form antibodies, new blood cells and neurotransmitters, which are brain chemicals that communicate information throughout your brain and body. It is vital to your baby's developing nervous system and brain. Research has also shown that extra vitamin B6 may relieve nausea and vomiting for some women during pregnancy.

Sources:

- Fish, poultry and lean meats.
- Chickpeas, brown rice, beans and nuts.
- Avocados, and prune juice.
- Fortified bread and cereals can also be a good source.

Vitamin C

Vitamin C is required for the collagen in connective tissue and, therefore, the developing foetal tissue and blood vessels, as well as bones. It is also necessary for assisting the body in absorbing iron and synthesising calcium. Studies have shown the importance of vitamin C to boost brain function. It has also been shown to be a potent antioxidant crucial for neutralising free radicals, helping to prevent colds and flu.

Sources:

- Leafy green vegetables like spinach, kale, watercress and Brussels sprouts, (preferably al dente).
- Citrus fruit, strawberries and blackcurrants are high in vitamin C, as are melons and papayas. Kiwi fruit actually contains more vitamin C than an orange! Guava not only has a high vitamin C content, it also contains folic acid, potassium and manganese, as well as being a rich source of fibre – a superfood indeed!

Vitamin D

Vitamin D helps your body absorb calcium which is important for both your bones and teeth, and that of your baby's too. It is also required for foetal development of the muscles, heart and nerves. It strengthens your immune system and let's not forget the feel good factor of getting out into the sunshine!

Sources:

- Sunlight is the main source of Vitamin D. It is synthesized in the epidermal layer of the skin when exposed to UVB radiation.

- Herring, sardines, salmon and mackerel.
- Button mushrooms, as well as shiitake mushrooms, especially when dried in the sun.

Other dietary essentials

Fibre

Fibre is essential for keeping your bowel regular and therefore, crucial in preventing constipation and haemorrhoids. During pregnancy your intestines shift to accommodate your growing baby and, along with the hormones that relax the muscles of the bowel, they may not work as efficiently. Also, if you are taking an iron supplement, it can make your stools dry and difficult to pass!

Sources:

- Fruit; prunes are especially helpful for constipation.
- Vegetables and legumes, such as lentils and black beans.
- Whole grain products like brown rice and wholemeal bread.

Also, remember to drink plenty of water as well as exercise regularly as this also helps move things along. You will know you have enough fibre and water in your diet if your stools are soft, large and well formed; floating stools are ideal!

Fat

There has been a lot of controversy in recent years around fat and it is important to remember that your body does require fats. Vitamins A, D, E, and K require fat in order to be transported around the body as they are fat-soluble vitamins. Fat also provides insulation and acts as a protective shield around vital organs like the liver, heart, and kidneys.

Saturated fat is considered the 'unhealthy' or 'bad' fat. It is a type of fat that is solid at room temperature mainly found in animal products such as dairy foods and meat, but can be found in some plant sources such as palm oil, cooking margarine, coconut milk and cream, and coconut products are generally beneficial during pregnancy in moderation. A lot of pre-packaged baked sweet products like biscuits and cakes, contain saturated fats and are best avoided.

Unsaturated fats are considered the 'healthy 'or 'good' fats and are liquid at room temperature. Essential fatty acids from omega-3 and omega-6 are unsaturated fats that can't be made in your body and therefore, must come from your diet.

Sources:

- Olive oil.
- Plant sources including linseed/flaxseed, walnuts, soybeans.
- Nuts and avocados.
- Fish, particularly oily fish such as salmon, sardines and Blue-eye, Travella (Cod).
- Eggs and meat, such as lean beef and chicken

Foods and drinks to avoid

Now that we have covered the dietary essentials to support your body and that of your developing baby, what foods should be avoided?

Alcohol:

- There is no safe recommendation for alcohol; medical experts advise abstinence during pregnancy.
- The main risk from drinking during pregnancy is your child developing foetal alcohol spectrum disorder. This syndrome can create problems with the baby's brain, causing developmental delays as well as facial abnormalities.

Caffeine

- Caffeine is a diuretic, which means it dehydrates the body by forcing fluid out in your urine. Coffee, tea and chocolate all contain caffeine, so it is best to limit your intake of all of these. Instead, drink plenty of water, or herbal teas without caffeine.

- If you are going to drink herbal teas, check that they are suitable during pregnancy. Liquorice tea for example, is contraindicated so please avoid it. Note - raspberry leaf tea is best avoided until the 36th week.

Foods at risk of containing harmful bacteria

In addition, avoid the following foods as they hold the risk of having harmful bacteria present such as listeria or salmonella:

- Raw fish — avoid sashimi, oysters, smoked salmon or smoked oysters and refrigerated ready-to-eat peeled prawns.
- Sushi rice is one of the most likely sources of food poisoning if left for long periods, so if you make your own, eat immediately and again, don't use any raw fish.
- Pâtés or meat spreads.
- Processed meats; ham, salami, chicken, luncheon meat, etc.
- Cold chicken or turkey used in sandwich bars.
- Soft and semi-soft cheeses like brie, camembert, feta, blue cheese and ricotta.
- Raw eggs: avoid homemade mayonnaise, aioli or chocolate mousse (some recipes use raw eggs).
- Pre-prepared or pre-packaged salads from a salad bar, including fruit salad.

A note on fish

While fish in your diet has many benefits, it is important to be careful as some fish may contain mercury at levels that may harm your baby's development. Aim for 2–3 servings per week (1 serving = 150 g), with the exception of catfish, deep sea perch, shark (flake) and billfish, like swordfish and marlin, of which you should only eat one serving per week with no other fish that week. Other species to limit are barramundi, gemfish, ling and tuna.

Choose ocean trout, salmon, sardines, herring, blue mackerel, anchovy, blue-eye cod, bream, flathead, garfish, whiting, mullet and snapper as these are some of the safest options. A general rule of thumb is that the larger the predatory fish, the more mercury. For further information check out www.foodauthority.nsw.gov.au and search 'pregnancy and food safety'.

In summary:

- Avoid processed foods and limit your intake of those foods that are low in nutritional value.
- As much as possible, eat fresh and organic.
- When eating out or getting a takeaway, be mindful of how the food you are consuming may have been prepared. Go for safe options that are supportive of your body and growing baby.
- Ensure you are well hydrated. Water is always the best option as juices can often contain lots of sugar without the benefit of the fibre of the original fruit.
- Limit your intake of caffeine, or cut it out completely.
- Remember that what you put into your body is important to you and your baby, yet don't stress and get too serious or obsessive. Treat yourself gently and nourish and nurture yourself with delicious, nutritious foods.

Figure 4.1 Nutrition

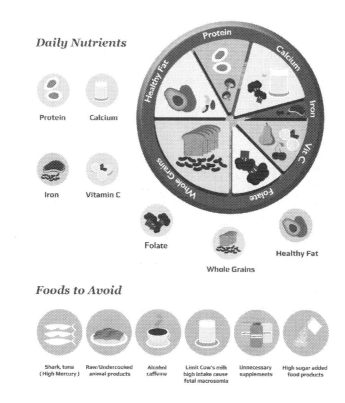

Chapter 5:
The birth process

You have within you right now, everything you need to deal with whatever the world can throw at you. – Brian Tracy.

The birth process demonstrates how amazing your body truly is, as you will see in this chapter. Your uterus is a muscle that, during the birthing process, contracts; firstly, to pull up and open the cervix and, secondly, push the baby down and out of the vagina. That is the basic mechanics of the birthing process, there is nothing difficult or mysterious about it!

Figure 5.1 Position of the baby in the body

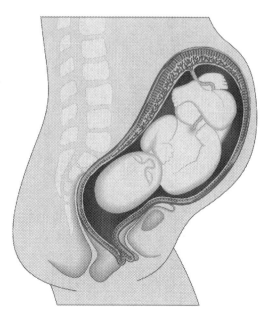

This chapter covers the origins of the medical model to birth and how that has created the birthing experience we commonly have in the West. I also look at what happens physiologically when your body goes into labour, the stages of labour, how stress affects the body during birth and the benefits of the relaxation response. Then we will look at how you can work with the birthing process. I will also discuss the very important role that the birthing partner plays, and give suggestions as to what he or she can do to best support the birthing mother during this wonderful transformative process. Then briefly, I will touch on Lotus birth and the potential benefits.

Origins of the medical approach to birth

It was during the seventeenth century that birth was redefined; science took over and the body was conceptualised as a machine. In the name of efficiency, birth became a process with stages, measurements and mechanisms. This is still what underpins modern-day obstetrics, as birth has now been split by the medical model into three separate stages, and within each stage are distinct phases as well.

Figure 5.2 The body viewed as a machine

The first stage of labour has three phases: latent, active and transitional. During this stage, the uterus has regular contractions and the cervix is dilating. The second stage commences once the cervix is fully dilated at ten cms and finishes once the baby is born. The third stage is from the birth of the baby, through to the delivery of the placenta and membranes, and finishes with control of bleeding. By breaking down birth into stages and phases, it then becomes a measurable structured event with markers to be achieved on an imposed time frame; creating limits and boundaries as to what is 'normal'.

Consequently, women have markers to achieve (e.g. to be dilating at around one centimetre an hour), and the pressure is on mothers to perform according to the textbook rather than going with the flow of their body. Birth is managed on a time frame when in a hospital setting and the individual is lost as the criteria has to be met. There is a tool called the partogram that is used in hospitals around the world by practitioners as a guideline for the progress of birth. This was originally based on Freidman's study in the 1950s where he plotted the cervical dilation of 100 women having their first baby in an American hospital. This was modified in the 1970s by Phillpott and Castle, who were creating guidelines to prevent poor outcomes in remote areas of Rhodesia in cases of obstructed labour. They added alert lines for when to transfer to hospital, as well as an action (augmentation) to Freidman's partogram.

A recent Cochrane review of the use of the partogram in labour has stated that: "On the basis of the findings of this review, we cannot recommend routine use of the partogram as part of standard labour management and care." This is because the time frames that have been laid down as normal by the partogram are not a true picture and that the cervix may take longer to dilate than the stated one centimetre per hour. By putting greater weight on the numbers, we risk losing the importance of focusing on the individual. While births do follow a certain sequence, no two women will have exactly the same experience. So it might be more useful to observe that mum and baby are fine and let nature take its course.

The consequence of the use of the partogram is that when a birthing woman deviates from what the medical institution considers 'normal', which current research shows to be an inaccurate picture, they will then have their births augmented. This could mean artificial rupture of membranes, in other words, having their water broken or being put on a syntocin drip. All of which may potentially increase their likelihood of requiring a caesarean. If these interventions do not increase the rate of cervical dilation, birthing women are then diagnosed with failure to progress. It can definitely be harder to relax if your thinking is focused on imagined problems, which then lead to feelings of fear, anxiety and pressure. Staying relaxed is pivotal to assist with the dilation of the cervix and allow you to deliver your baby with ease.

With fewer than 50 percent of women meeting the narrow criteria of 'normal progress' as first-time mums, it is unlikely that they would be able to avoid having their labour augmented. The World Health Organization estimates that the actual rate of obstructed labour is only between 3 to 6 percent worldwide, which suggests that many women experience unnecessary intervention during their labour.

I am curious as to why some of the opportunities for women to have a natural birth are not promoted. Birth can be an experience with transformational properties and yet there is so much underlying fearful thinking around the birthing process. Another, less discussed, factor is that doctors must practice a certain number of techniques during their time in obstetrics in order to qualify. This means that they are looking for opportunities to perform interventions with each delivery and *not* opportunities to create a natural birthing experience for couples. It is important that women and their partners step into their own power and take responsibility for the birth plan of their baby.

Going into labour

Labour commences in different ways for each woman and even then, for each birth. Some women experience what is delightfully termed a 'bloody show', which is usually a pink or blood-stained jelly-like loss. This is when the mucus plug comes away, and is an indication that your cervix is starting to open up. It can be clear, pink, or blood-tinged and as it is thick vaginal discharge, not all women will recognise it or possibly, even notice it. Although it is an indication that your body is moving towards labour, it could be minutes, hours or days before the onset of your labour.

For others, a regular rhythmic contraction signals that labour has begun. This is not to be confused with Braxton Hicks, which are irregular, or their regularity is not maintained for long spells; they also seldom last more than one minute. You may feel the first labour contractions as a backache. To begin with, contractions will often be short in duration, 30 to 40 seconds and may be as much as half an hour apart.

Another indication is when your 'waters break'. This is when the amniotic sac, surrounding the foetus, ruptures and there is a leak of amniotic fluid. This is commonly dramatised in the movies but statistically only experienced by one in 12 births. Upon rupture the amniotic fluid should be clear and odourless, and while the reasons are not fully understood, it usually happens while you are sleeping. It may be a sudden gush or you may simply notice a constant trickle.

If this does occur, pop in a sanitary pad and observe if the fluid is clear and odourless or discoloured.

- If you do notice any discolouration, especially if it is green or smells, contact your healthcare provider.
- If it is clear and odourless, you have just had an indication that the birthing process will soon begin. It may happen imminently, in a few hours or possibly, days. Let those involved in your birth know what has happened and rest assured that your body is in the process of changing and readying for the birthing journey.

During the birthing process, the body releases specialised hormones, such as oxytocin and endorphins to ease and prepare your body for the changes that are part of birth. The hormone relaxin plays a particularly important role during pregnancy in that it allows the body's muscles, joints and ligaments to relax in order to accommodate the growing baby. Its effects are also seen during the birthing, in the relaxing of the pelvic ligaments and the softening of the cervix.

The stages of labour

In the first stage of labour, the cervix softens and ripens. What does this mean? The cervix is the opening to the uterus and is positioned at the top of the vagina. During pregnancy, the cervix remains closed with the opening blocked by the mucous plug, as mentioned earlier. The cervix begins to 'ripen' in preparation for the birth; the water content increases and the cervix becomes softer and more vascular. These changes enable it to stretch, thin and then dilate to the magic 10 centimetres.

Figure 5.3 The first stage of labour — the cervix dilating

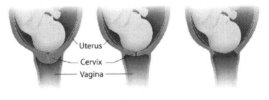

1. Before labour   2. Ripening & opening,   3. Fully dilated
1cm dilated   to 10cm

As labour progresses, the waves of contractions get longer in duration and closer together. If it begins at night, you can rest and maybe doze your way through; if during the day, you might want to potter with minor jobs or something you enjoy, maybe even going for a gentle walk if the mood takes you. The traditional old wives tale of scrubbing the steps of the house when labour starts is an interesting idea, as it puts the woman on all fours. This position can assist a posterior baby to move into an anterior position – baby's spine away from yours. Gravity can help the spine to move from the back, near or next to the mother's spine (posterior position) and around to the side or the front of the bump (anterior), which is the optimum position for birthing.

I love the analogy of contractions as being like waves because, just like the shape of a wave, they start low and then rise incrementally upwards until they peak and then fall back down again. During birthing, you are riding the waves; you can't stop them, though you can learn how to ride them.

'Transition' is the term given when your cervix has reached seven to ten centimetres in dilation. This can sometimes be an intense emotional experience for some women on their birthing journey. Some even vomit, which many birth attendants see as a good sign, as it may indicate that your baby's arrival is imminent! However, this is the exception and not the rule. By being in the zone, where you are relaxed and calm, you greatly decrease the minimal odds of vomiting.

The second stage of labour begins when the cervix is fully dilated and ends with the delivery of your baby.

During the waves of contractions the uterine muscle pulls up on the sides of the cervix, encouraging it to open, while simultaneously pushing the baby down and into the birth canal to create pressure on the cervix to open even further. It is important to focus on breathing deeply, using your diaphragm and abdomen to pull more air into your lungs, and not just breathe from your chest.

Figure 5.4 The second stage of labour — the birth of the baby

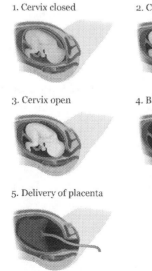

1. Cervix closed   2. Cervix opening

3. Cervix open   4. Baby being born

5. Delivery of placenta

You can practice this deep and even breathing technique every day throughout your pregnancy. That will help it to become second nature for you and you will be prepared for when you go into labour. Gently place one hand on top of your beautiful bump, consciously engage your diaphragm, and ensure that your bump moves upwards when you inhale and down when you exhale. This also helps to train the brain into an alpha brainwave state that is ideal for labour.

During labour, keep your breathing deep and even all the way through the contraction which, just like a wave, rises gently to its peak and then back down again. Once the wave has passed, there is a gap. Use this gap to notice if you are holding any tension anywhere in your body. Pay particular attention to the jaw, neck and shoulders, as these are the most common places for tension to be held. Imagine deeply breathing in love and then blowing any tension away with a longer breath out. Focus on relaxing and releasing to avoid wasting energy with tension. This will assist you to be deeply relaxed and ready to ride the next wave with ease.

When should I go to the hospital?

If you are birthing in the hospital it is important to not arrive too early, as being in hospital can sometimes slow the birthing process down for many women. Additionally, once you are in the hospital system, you are then often under pressure to perform in a certain amount of time, as designated by hospital protocols. This can cause unnecessary stress. A general guide to follow is when your contractions are about five minutes apart and lasting around one minute in length, then contact the healthcare provider where you are booked in to have your baby.

When I teach my classes, I talk to couples about imagining labouring comfortably at home and arriving at the hospital or the birth centre at around eight cm dilated. Trust your intuition. If you feel the need to go to hospital, then follow your body's wisdom.

The truth is, your body knows exactly what to do. Childbirth doesn't have to be a painful process that must be endured, as we have been told. Ask your angels for strength and guidance during your birthing. While birth is a physical experience, at some points you may feel restless or have doubts about your ability. It is nothing you cannot handle. The human race would have otherwise died out! Tune into all the other women birthing at the same time along with you, around the planet, to give you strength and know that you are never alone.

Focus on relaxing and riding the waves. By applying the deep breathing technique discussed earlier this will help you to relax. This will diminish the possibility of triggering a stress response in your body. If you have ever seen a panic attack or experienced one yourself, you may have noticed that the breathing is shallow and only coming from the chest area, not the deep diaphragmatic breathing discussed here.

Once you hit transition and you are at the magic ten centimetres, sometimes called the second stage, you may experience a shift in energy and feel a strong sensation and desire to 'push'. Occasionally birthing mothers feel like they want to vomit as I mentioned earlier and when they do, it can be a great relief and release. This is nothing to be alarmed about. Some women experience a period of respite where everything seems to stop before the desire to push kicks in. Please refrain from panic and enjoy the rest.

If everything is fine with your baby, such as the heart rate, it indicates that there are no special circumstances, so allow the process to unfold at its own pace.

There can be pressure to move this process along, from the medical staff, due to hospital policies or fear. They may recommend medical interventions such as episiotomies, suction or forceps. Again, if everything is fine with both you and the baby, you can apply the old adage of 'if it isn't broken, don't fix it'. Your body has a natural expulsive reflex, which gives you the sensation of wanting to push. The waves may come less frequently than before, and are far more expulsive, as is their design.

Sometimes you may experience a strong wave, followed by a lesser one and then back to a stronger one. This is also normal. This a great time to focus on the affirmation of 'Pleasure, is opening up for my baby' as you continue to breathe deeply with the urge to push. Do not hold your breath. Instead, use your breath to engage your diaphragm to assist your uterus with the gentle expulsion of your baby.

Transition can be a very empowering process as beta-endorphins flow through your system. These are the body's naturally occurring opiates. It can almost feel like an otherworldly experience; you feel the high and euphoria of your body's chemistry as well as the sensation of bringing your baby into the world, with you as both a Goddess and a Creator.

It is no wonder that this story has been quashed by society; to see women in such a divine light can be threatening to the status quo. So instead we have been sold a story of pain and anguish, that our bodies are somehow flawed and that birth is inherently dangerous. I am telling this story, like many women before me, so that we can take back our power that we have relinquished to others. We can empower our experience through birth, which creates strength, deeper self-love and appreciation for this miracle that we are all a part of.

The third stage of birth begins with the birth of your baby and completes with the delivery of the placenta. In a hospital setting they often have a policy of a managed third stage. The focus is on prevention of haemorrhaging, or blood loss, by intervention. This may mean an injection of syntocinon in the upper portion of your thigh; which encourages the uterus to contract and expel the placenta.

In contrast, a natural third stage is where you have the baby skin to skin, and your focus is on your baby. This helps your body release the natural version of syntocinon – oxytocin – the 'love drug'. Breastfeeding your baby also stimulates the release of oxytocin. And, with oxytocin stimulating the uterus to contract, the placenta is birthed.

It is also now considered best practice in England to wait for the umbilical cord connecting your baby to the placenta to stop pulsating, before clamping and cutting it. This allows oxygenated and nutrient rich blood to pass through the placenta to the baby.

This last stage, the delivery of the amazing placenta, can take anywhere from 5 to 20 minutes but can be up to an hour. You may feel mild contractions as the placenta separates from the uterine wall and into the birth canal where it may take one or two gentle pushes to expel it completely. Sometimes the midwife or obstetrician will massage with gentle pressure on your uterus (by massaging your lower abdomen) to assist the uterus to contract. They may also pull gently on the cord to extract the placenta once it has released from the uterine wall.

The placenta and membranes are then checked by your midwife or obstetrician thoroughly, to make sure it has all come away and is completely intact. They will also check your perineum and vagina to ensure that everything is fine and see if any stitching is required. While there are many factors involved, staying relaxed during the birth can minimise vaginal tearing. I was delighted to discover it was indeed possible for me to have a 'big' baby and everything remained intact. No stitches required.

Please remember to pause to be present with this amazing new life you have nurtured and brought into this world. It's good to be aware that this is your baby's first introduction to life on planet earth and this new environment! This time is special. Allow some time for you and your partner to welcome your baby into this new world; skin to skin is ideal during these first moments. Hold off anything that is non-essential like washing, weights and measures.

Enjoy and savour this triumph; you have your beautiful baby in your arms. Congratulate yourself on this amazing and miraculous conclusion of one experience, and realise it is the beginning of a new and exciting chapter of your life.

How stress affects the birthing body

'Fear is the energy which contracts, closes down, draws in, runs, hides, hoards, harms. Love is the energy which expands, opens up, sends out, reveals, shares, heals.' — Neil Donald Walsch

Stress is a major problem with today's fast pace; it is a common complaint and has many implications for health. While the body is designed to cope with stress in short bursts, long term it can be detrimental and studies suggest that it contributes to the disease process.

What about the stress women feel about birth? Stress creates a physiological response in the body. It is important to remember that while the stressor can be real or imagined, in either situation your body will still create the stress (or fight-or-flight) response.

When you think of all the potential areas that might cause stress, these may not even be at a conscious level, gently switch to a positive thought. Hospitals, usually, have negative associations, after all it is where you go if you are sick, or have had an accident. I have worked in many hospitals over the years and even I'm not overly keen on them! To make no mention of that unmistakable hospital smell!

Everyone has scary thoughts from time to time. Your concerns can range from labour pains and whether you think you will be able to handle them, or the possibility of something going wrong, to worries about how you will fare as a parent and how being a mum or dad may affect your relationships, career, finances, and the list goes on and on. I'll stop before I scare you! These are most of the usual fears that I have come across in my many years as a birthing mentor, so rest assured this is all perfectly normal.

Be aware that many of these fears are never actually realised and you can let them go. They can become a source of torture and torment. They are not real, merely the Principle of Thought taking form in the moment. Or as I like to think of it, going down the tunnel with no cheese! These thoughts, real or imagined will create the stress response. When that happens, the body responds ready to fight or take flight; releasing adrenaline, cortisol and other hormones into the bloodstream, which instruct certain blood vessels to constrict and others to dilate so that blood flow is shunted to where it is needed most to aid running away or fighting.

This causes increased blood flow to the legs and arms and the pupils dilate to let in more light; digestion is not deemed essential at this time, nor is the uterus. This compromises blood flow, lowers the level of oxygen in the uterus which can increase the level of uterine discomfort during labour. British obstetrician, Grantly Dick Read, observed this process as fear, tension, and pain. With the increase in adrenaline, the hormone that causes contractions to generate, oxytocin, drops.

Now this is all very well and good if there is a real, life-threatening emergency as this response mechanism is there to preserve our lives. Our ancient ancestors may have found themselves in a situation where the ability to press pause on labour was key to their survival; had a sabre tooth tiger appeared, immediate flight would have been necessary to ensure their safety. Yet today the perceived fears and anxieties, and the subsequent biological responses, increase discomfort during labour and work against the birthing body.

Fear, tension and pain can create a Failure To Progress (FTP), as labelled by the medical profession. When the cervix doesn't dilate to the magic 10 centimetres according to the partogram, then FTP may be diagnosed, which then dictates intervention according to hospital policies. Your oxygen consumption then increases and breathing becomes more rapid, as does your heart rate.

Is it any wonder that there is a cycle of fear that is self-perpetuating? A cycle or loop feeds back into itself; obsessive thoughts, worry and negative emotions can then create increased tension which may lead to an increase in pain. This can become a cycle which leads to increased fear and anxiety, more tension, and again leads to increased discomfort. This cycle can continue until interrupted, and it is best if never allowed to start in the first place.

The relaxation response

Fortunately, there is an antidote to the stress response and potential fear cycle. It is aptly named 'the relaxation response'. The relaxation response has always existed in the context of religious teachings and is a widespread practice in Eastern cultures with meditation. It is also elicited through hypnosis, which is a wonderful tool to amplify your focus on comfort and relaxation.

Current research proves that focusing on relaxation decreases pain. The relaxation response slows the heart rate and breathing, and decreases muscle tension. When I worked in the operating theatre, during some of my breaks, I used a pulse oximeter, which is a device which gently clips onto the fingertip to measure oxygen levels and pulse rate. I observed how, by taking slow deep breaths, I could visibly bring my pulse rate down.

Meditation, hypnosis and yoga are a few of the different, and more commonly known, tools to get you into the relaxation zone. If you are able to practice these techniques well in advance of going into labour you will be able to easily create the relaxation response when you are experiencing the stimulus of birth. This releases endorphins that bond to pain receptor sites in your body and ensure that you are on a feedback loop that brings more relaxation and comfort. Other relaxing and nurturing options such as massage, listening to music, walking in nature, swimming, yoga and other forms of gentle exercise are all great methods for eliminating stress and aiding sleep. Your wisdom will guide you to your ideal form of relaxing.

As you relax and focus on breathing slowly and deeply, muscle tension decreases and blood flows easily to the highly vascular uterine muscle. Sensations of the muscle contracting are then experienced as tightening or pressure and in ease. This releases endorphins which increases relaxation, prevents tension and, what may have been labeled as pain, is decreased. Using the relaxation response will help you work with your birthing body, allowing you to relax and open with ease.

One of my favourite affirmations that I used during the birth of my son, Ben, was 'pleasure is opening up for my baby'. I focused on relaxing and consciously releasing any tension in my muscles. By releasing muscle tension, you are also minimising the risk of the potential of tearing, one of the main fears that I hear about. Ben was a ten pound baby and I feel that my focus on relaxing and working with my body enabled me to deliver him without intervention.

The stimulus of birth is inevitable and how you choose to respond will either help or potentially hinder the process — therein lies your growth and freedom. I suspect you agree it is important to prepare yourself and practice, so that it is second nature and your relaxation response is automatic.

I hope you now see that relaxation isn't a luxury, it's a necessity to better health and birthing. Also remember to purposefully create time to relax after you have your baby. It will really help you to be at your best, and this will have a flow-on effect to everyone around you. By ensuring you nurture yourself, and allow others to nurture you, you will be able to, in turn, nurture your newborn.

How to work with your body during labour

'Our deepest fear is not that we are inadequate. Our deepest fear is that we are powerful beyond measure.' — Marianne Williamson

Birth is a physiological process that has now become in our culture, synonymous with pain, difficulty, failure and fear. Yet in its most simplistic form it is just a muscle contracting. That is all the uterus is, a muscle.

Every other function of our body does not cause pain unless there is a problem. So perhaps if discomfort is experienced during childbirth, it brings with it all the fears that have grown in our collective Western apprehensions about birth.

There is a popular story that childbirth is painful and yet, what is not part of cultural narrative as yet is that women are strong.

What I have learnt from my 50 years on this wonderful planet — which has been underlined by the experience of birth — is the importance of trusting, surrendering and allowing life to unfold. Not always an easy thing to do! However, this is one of the reasons I was inspired to write this book. This approach is extremely important during birth and then this truth ripples out to the rest of your life, and subsequently, the world.

Trusting the process of birth and knowing that both your body and your baby are designed perfectly to birth, every wave (contraction) is bringing your baby closer to being in your arms. When you work with the process of birth, you support your body in releasing the wonderful hormones and endorphins, and allow your birthing body to take over.

Birth is really about being in the present moment, not stuck in the past or projecting into the future. There is only now, and by stressing about how long it might take and whether you can cope (which are all future projections), you may miss the power of the present moment.

Your breath is one of the best tools to keep you centred in the now, and when used purposefully, it helps you to remain in a state of calm and relaxation, not to mention that it ensures that your uterus and baby are receiving plenty of oxygenated blood. During each wave, the uterus rises. Deep breathing also engages your diaphragm so that during a contraction, this deep and slow breathing assists to pull the uterus up. Thus working with your birthing body, making each wave more effective and efficient, your breathing also helps you access a deeper state of relaxation.

When someone experiences panic, their rate of breathing quickens and they breathe from their chest alone. This quick shallow breathing is prevalent in panic attacks. Women, in general, tend to be more shallow breathers, so it is important to engage your diaphragm to breathe deeply. Have a practice now. Notice your normal rate and depth of breathing and now focus on breathing fully and deeply. That's right, engage your diaphragm too. Do this for a minute or so and connect with how you feel when you deepen and lengthen your breath.

It's amazing how breath can create a state of relaxation, just by such a simple and easy technique of breathing deeply and fully. It changes your brainwave to the alpha state, synonymous with relaxation. It is no coincidence that meditation, hypnosis, yoga and also birthing all use the breath to relax, and to keep your focus in the present moment. So just as in meditation, during your birthing, keep bringing yourself back to your breath and the present moment. It really is that simple!

Swiss psychologist, Carl Jung, said:, "What we resist, persists." By trusting the process, with whatever twists and turns your birthing may take, you are able to be in a state of allowing, rather than resisting. When things don't go quite according to your ideal plan, take some time to examine it. Do not allow yourself to be rushed, either internally with spiraling negative thoughts or externally to outside pressure. If you find yourself feeling uncertain, you can always take a moment to collect your thoughts and allow Divine wisdom to lead the way.

'Don't rush to decide what to do. Intend to let Divine inspiration flow to, and it will be so.' Christine Northrup, MD

How can you work with the process?

It is important to focus your mind on how you want your birthing experience to unfold and remember that what you focus on expands!

- Keep your mind focused on your afformations or affirmations.
- Notice where you are comfortable in your body and what positions aid your comfort and relaxation.
- Trust in your body to birth; you have an innate ability and it is important you relax into that and have certainty within yourself, just as I have absolute certainty in your ability.
- Take time to use and focus on your breath!

Birth positions

During the birthing process, there are many positions to help facilitate your labour. You don't have to go through every position known to women — go with only what works for you. It will also depend on when you go into labour. If at night, going for a walk may not be the best option! Stay in bed and get into any position which you find most comfortable. Focus on deep breathing and do your best to catch some sleep between waves, unless you feel restless and need to get up and walk about your home. Use your early labour to engage and relax into the process.

During the day, in the early stages it can be nice to go for a walk. Gravity and movement all help with the process so it doesn't have to be far or at a fast pace! With my second labour, we took our daughter to our local park. It was great to get out into nature and enjoy family time before the upcoming change in dynamics. Alternatively, you could potter around your home getting those last minute jobs completed.

Hip rocking is great when you are standing still; remember to have a slight bend in your knees, with your feet shoulder-width apart. This can be done on a birthing ball, leaning on a mantelpiece or placing your arms around your partner's neck and allowing your upper body to relax as you circle your hips. Your partner can also have their hands on your hips gently helping you with the rocking motion.

I attended one lady who spent a lot of her labour with her upper body resting on the sofa seat with her knees on the floor, gently rotating her hips. Just make sure to place a cushion under your knees to maintain comfort. This position is not too far away from being on all fours; again, ensure comfort for the knees and also the hands, when on all fours.

A practice that was encouraged long ago was to have the labouring mother scrub the steps of the house. Now I'm not saying this is a time to start scrubbing floors! However, I think the reason this has become an old wive's tale in England is that this puts the birthing mother on her hands and knees and allows gravity to assist the baby's spine to come to the front of the bump. A number of us today spend a lot of our time sitting at computers, watching television and alike, which doesn't always create comfort for the hips or give the maximum benefits that being on all fours can.

If your baby is in a posterior position, you can remain on your knees, drop the front of your body down onto your forearms so that your bottom is higher than your shoulders and head. This encourages the baby to turn to an anterior position which is the ideal position for birth.

Both swimming regularly and using a belly bean bag with a hole in it for your bump, allow gravity to assist moving your baby to an optimal position for birth. Some massage therapists who specialise in pregnancy massage have tables designed with a hole allowing you to lay face down. What a great way to pamper your pregnant body and help get or maintain your baby in the best position. You can also add the affirmation 'my baby is in the ideal position for birth' to your daily routine.

Most hospitals and birth centres have birthing balls, otherwise known as exercise balls, as they have been found to be a great place to sit and labour. You can just sit on them and use the ball to rotate your hips round in a circular movement.

Some women find it comfortable to spend some time labouring on the toilet. Obviously you will need to change the venue once the baby's head is visible and starting to crown.

Birthing stools are also a great option for both labour and for the delivery. The position is meant to open up the hips and the design allows easy access for the midwife to receive the baby, so there would be no need to get up and move when you are in the zone. Squatting is another option as it also opens the hips; place your feet flat on the floor with your weight on your heels. Depending on your level of stamina, this position may not be something you can maintain for long periods of time. Having support from your birthing partner who can hold you, and allow you to lean on them, will help. Prenatal yoga can help you prepare for labour; the poses designed for the latter stages of pregnancy help to improve your body's flexibility and strengthen you to be able to hold those positions during labour and delivery.

If you choose to lie on your side, place an extra pillow between your legs or have someone support your upper leg to keep your thighs apart as that helps, or avoids, hip or back discomfort. Lying on the left hand side encourages better blood flow to the uterus. Some women find that lying down, especially in the latter stages of the birthing process, can sometimes make back pain more intense. If you choose to lie on your back, sitting nearly upright with plenty of pillows for support encourages the baby to descend, whereas lying on your side does not use gravity to its full effect. With that being said, during my second labour, after being active for much of the day, I went to bed at night. When I did transfer to the birth centre, I spent quite a while in bed relaxing on my side with my husband, before I transferred to the bath when I felt birth was imminent.

Once in the birth pool, you can change positions with ease; either floating on all fours or lying on your back with your body supported against the wall of the bath. With the pressure of gravity off and the soothing warmth of the water, I found it to be the ideal place to engage the relaxation response and give birth gently. Your baby doesn't draw its first breath until it comes in contact with air. I loved sitting in the warm bath with my newly born baby on my chest. It is a choice that you will need to plan ahead for. If you want a water birth and you are planning on birthing at home, you will need to rent an approved birth pool. Many hospitals and birth centres are now equipped with birthing baths. It would be wise to discuss your wish to birth in water, as some facilities may either ask you to get out or drain the bath when birth is imminent.

When thinking about having a water birth; if you enjoy baths and usually find them relaxing then a water birth may be a good option for you. If on the other hand you don't like baths, then a water birth might not be the right fit for you. The other thing to know with birthing in water is that it is often recommended to use the bath towards the end of your labouring.

As I said before, go with what feels comfortable, helps you relax and stay focused on your breathing, while maintaining the flow of the birthing process. Find the positions that work for you and support the progress of your labour. Unless you go into labour in the middle of the night and prefer instead to rest, allow gravity to assist you in the earlier stages. Enjoy the freedom to move and choose what feels right at the time. For the final crowning phase, if lying on your back, ensure that you are resting just above the tailbone so as to allow your pelvis to open and not to impede the baby's impending birth. No two births are the same; your birth experience will be unique to you. This also applies to any subsequent labours, as you learn and grow in your understanding and knowledge of your body's capabilities.

Lotus Birth

Lotus Birth was named after Claire Lotus Day who, in 1974, birthed her son in hospital and took him home with his placenta still attached. She had observed chimpanzees doing this and felt they were more content. She attributed this to feeling secure, with their placenta still tethered to them. So she chose to test the theory with her next birth! Although Lotus Birth is seen as quite a new tradition, ancient cultures have practiced leaving the baby and placenta attached.

A Lotus Birth involves leaving the baby's cord and placenta attached until the cord dries out and then detaches of its own accord, instead of the usual practice of clamping and cutting immediately after birth. It can take around three to 10 days to dry up and fall off, which is a similar timeline if the cord had been clamped and cut.

Why bother with a Lotus Birth?

This isn't going to be everyone's choice, as it means the added dimension of carrying the placenta in a bag until it naturally detaches from your baby. We had a beautiful blue velvet bag made for this purpose. This extra consideration can make the usual everyday outings a little trickier, so support of friends and relatives is very helpful. You can also prepare in advance by making freezer dinners, as to go shopping and getting back into the hurly burly of life is best avoided in early postpartum.

I noticed with my second child that due to choosing a Lotus Birth, I didn't go anywhere until Ben's placenta detached naturally at 10 days. This was a wonderfully different experience compared to the frenetic activity of going to show Lauren off at a friend's party two days after her birth!

This slower, quieter approach was much more healing for me, allowing the time to bond with my newborn, as opposed to wanting to show him off like I did with Lauren. I wished I had known about the Lotus Birth option for her. With hindsight, those first few days with your baby are very precious and showing them off can wait, as that phase of being proud of your creation never ends.

I remember being far more emotional when my milk came in with Lauren, and generally less chilled out, possibly due to all the running around after her birth. It may have been from being a first-time mother as well as the different seasons in which they were born. It's always easier to stay indoors in the winter as opposed to the summer. I suppose I'll never know for sure. I now always recommend to my mothers-to-be to take it slowly after the birth, just as they do in other cultures. A Lotus Birth really encourages this!

A Lotus Birth also ensures that you have a natural third stage of labour, no injection of syntocinon to assist the uterus to contract and expel the placenta. Again we are honouring the natural process of birth, without intervention. This also means the cord isn't clamped and cut immediately after delivery, and ensures that the baby receives maximum blood volume.

The baby's immature liver continues to be supported by the placenta in the offloading of toxins after delivery until detaching from the uterine wall. The baby receives the full contents of the cord, plus an extra 40 to 60 millilitres of blood from the placenta. The blood is highly nutritious and fully oxygenated, containing stem cells, iron, hormones and enzymes.

This is all lost when the traditional immediate clamping and cutting of the cord takes place. When you consider that this is the equivalent of 1200 millilitres of blood loss for an adult, that is a lot of blood volume for the newborn to make up in their first hours after birth. Around one-third of the baby's total blood volume in fact. Fortunately, delayed cord cutting (DCC) is building in momentum, and has been taken on as standard practice in England now. It still has to be requested in Australia, despite the research of the benefits. It can take the medical establishment a long time to catch up with the current research.

Shivam Rachana, in her book *Lotus Birth*, talks of the benefits from an energetic point of view, which Western medicine does not really consider. She states that Lotus Birth cares for the subtle energetic bodies — the aura and chakras — which are mapped out and well understood in Eastern philosophies and healthcare systems. The navel chakra is the major energy centre in the body; Lotus Birth allows this chakra to be undisturbed, and has been shown to have major benefits to the child's ongoing health.

Lotus Birth requires a few practical logistics. Shortly after birth, you will need to drain the placenta, pat dry, then salt and wrap it in traditional cloth nappies and place into a specially made outer bag. You will need to carry your baby and placenta until the cord detaches at the umbilicus. The placenta will need to be re-salted, as the salt helps to dry it thus diminishing odours, and the cloth nappies changed. You can also add herbs or lavender oils to sweeten the aroma. So you have to be willing to do this or get a doula to help with this process daily at first and then every second day until the placenta detaches.

Ben's placenta was called my 'bagpipe' as I carried it under my arm while holding, changing or transferring him around. My lovely husband found the whole thing very awkward, though he was willing to indulge my wishes. He was certainly relieved when it fell off! When choosing a Lotus Birth, you must be prepared for a little added extras. I really felt that it was all definitely worthwhile. My doula, Jasmine, came and attended to the placenta and it was always a joy to see her again. I was also able to have Ben skin to skin for a lot longer when he was first born, while the placenta was drained, prepared and wrapped.

My experience

I did not hear of Claire Lotus Day until I had done my doula training and began to immerse myself deeply into the more natural approaches to birth. It made sense to me and I was keen that my next birth would be Lotus. But I'm getting ahead of myself; the story begins earlier while I was attending a doula gathering at Denise Love's centre. In walked Jasmine, who was calling herself a spiritual midwife, and had come to enquire about doula training. I walked over to her at the end of the meeting and told her that she really must do the training as I wanted her as my doula, even though I wasn't even pregnant at the time! She probably thought I was a little crazed, or maybe a lot! I didn't see Jasmine again until well over a year later when we met again at another doula gathering, this time I was heavily pregnant with Ben. I was confident in my ability to birth and had been thinking about having a Lotus Birth but hadn't yet done anything about it. Jasmine told me that she was now working as a doula and specialised in Lotus Births. I asked her if she would be willing to come to Ben's birth to facilitate this aspect and I'm glad to say I got the Lotus Birth for Ben that I desired. I would definitely recommend exploring Lotus Birth to see if you feel this might be an option for you. This is totally a personal choice.

The partner's role

There had been some controversy as to whether there was a place for the father in the birthing room. It is only fairly recently that dad has been invited into the birthing suite! My own father wasn't present for my birth, despite him wanting to be there. Yet, now that they are able to be in the room, we expect that they will know what to do. (Expectation is always a recipe for disaster as it often creates an experience of disappointment.) Given that many women don't know what to do during birth, why do we assume that our birthing partner should know what to do? Especially when we consider that there are fewer opportunities now to see birth at home.

Your birthing partner is your advocate and supporter during the birth process.

It is really important that your birthing partner is fully present. So silence mobile phones, put down iPads so that they may be fully present for this miraculous event. As a birthing partner, their role is also to ensure that any interventions are not done unnecessarily or just as routine. They can ask the healthcare professionals, on your behalf, for the reason behind any suggestions for intervention. For example, vaginal examinations can be refused, as they are often done just as routine.

The following points will also assist your birthing partner with their role:

- Go through the birth plan together, well in advance of the due date, so that you have fully discussed and are aware of all your options, including your preferences if a special circumstance changes things. (See Chapter 6 for your birth plan.) Expect the best and be prepared for all eventualities. Nobody wants to be like the Titanic, so convinced as to its own invincibility that it didn't have enough lifeboats!
- Monitor the time between and the duration of her contractions, but do so intermittently to avoid it being the focus whereby you

are no longer present for her. To begin with, when contractions are regularly coming, time them every hour or so; as the contractions lengthen in duration and come more regularly, change this to every half an hour.

- Let the healthcare provider know when labour has begun. Once contractions are well established and lasting around a minute in length and about five minutes apart, consider going to hospital or the birth centre unless you've both organised a home birth.

- If birthing at home, give your midwife the information over the phone of the length and duration of the contractions. Once the midwife has arrived, you don't need to keep monitoring.

- Be observant for any signs of tension, usually visible in either the shoulders that rise upwards and are stiff, or possibly the clenching of her teeth and tension around the jaw. Remember relaxed mouth equals relaxed cervix! Lovingly suggest for her to relax her shoulders and/or jaw. Alternatively, gently apply light pressure to her shoulders while affirming for her to relax and let the tension go. Get her to focus on breathing fully and deeply.

- Whisper her favourite affirmations gently in her ear and provide verbal encouragement. Who doesn't enjoy and benefit from reassurance that they are doing well? Say, 'Well done, you are doing really well' or my personal favourite from my first doula, Gwen, 'You're a legend!' It still makes me smile to this day.

- Ensure good hydration by offering water regularly and assist her to the toilet. This is important because anatomically a full bladder can hinder the baby's descent so water in and water out!

- Help your partner change positions regularly to maintain optimum comfort. Ask her if she is in a comfortable position and if not, help her to move. Try hip rocking by facing her and placing her arms around your neck and then use your hands to support and rotate her hips. This can add comfort and give her strength from your energy and physical closeness.

- Gently stroke her skin with your fingertips to release endorphins and relax her more deeply. Touch is a great way to support her, especially when she is turning inward and not wanting to talk. (I had a client who for most of her labour had her partner caress her feet with great effect. When he asked his partner if he could stop because he was getting a bit tired, he received an emphatic NO!)

- Keep it positive! This is not the time for you to complain about being tired or hungry. You do have the easier job so suck it up! Be the best birthing partner you can be and keep your focus on how you can best support her during the birth of your baby. Thus ensuring she remembers your part in the birth for the right reasons!

- Have easy and nutritious snacks available for you both to keep energy up. Bananas, nuts and chopped carrots provide sustained energy, and are easy to eat. Avoid chocolate and sweets with their potential sugar spike and crash. Once mum is in the full swing of labour, she is unlikely to feel hungry and you will need to sustain yourself.

- Have the music that you both like organised as well as a hypnosis recording to aid focus. The most suitable music is that which soothes and relaxes. Ensure good ambience in the room to create a relaxing atmosphere; for example, soft lighting, and a comfortable room temperature.

- Let the staff know if you wish to announce the gender of your baby.

- The staff also need to know ahead of time, your plans for the cord. Whoever cuts the cord, the best practice is to wait until the cord has stopped pulsating before cutting and clamping.

In my role, I have witnessed a lot of wonderfully happy dads who really felt part of the birth process. When done well, a fully supportive partner provides the mother with the knowledge that everything is being taken care of and in turn, she can relax and birth. One couple that I have worked with springs to mind as I write this, Wade and Jess. The midwife commented to her student attending the birth that not only was the student lucky to have seen such an amazing birth, Wade was the best birthing partner the midwife had ever seen. He was mindfully watching and ensuring that Jess was using deep breathing to keep her focused and relaxed. He used light touch and massage to reassure, support and comfort her. She knew that she didn't have to think about anything; he had everything handled. He made sure she was drinking regularly and emptying her bladder too. All of his care, focus and attention helped to deepen her relaxation further and work with her birthing body.

A bit of knowledge can go a long way, so remain calm, keep your focus on your role and you too can be a birthing partner legend like Wade. Remember to enjoy the miracle that you are both a part of!

In summary, mum:

- Remember that your body is amazing and designed to birth your baby.
- Ride the waves of birth with your breath, deep and full all the way through each wave of the uterus contracting. Then in the gap between the waves, blow away any tension with a long out breath and deep inhalation. Imagine a wave of relaxation flowing down through your body, releasing and relaxing all your muscles.
- Choose positions you find comfortable, sway your hips with the waves if it feels good.
- Trust your body and stay at home until your contractions are around five minutes apart and lasting for around the one minute mark before transferring to the hospital or birth centre. Trust your innate wisdom as to when to transfer.
- Tune into all the other women birthing with you at this time. Tap into the collective strength and ask your angels for their help too.
- When you feel like pushing, use your diaphragm to nudge along with your breath to ease your baby out. You have a natural expulsive reflex. "Pleasure is opening up for my baby. Every wave brings my baby closer to my arms."
- Once you are holding your baby in your arms, savour the moment, remembering these first skin-to-skin moments are essential to creating a gentle beginning for your baby. Delay clamping the cord and get skin-to-skin with this wonderful miracle, your baby, which you have created.

Chapter 6:
Plan for the worst and expect the best

We are built to conquer the environment, solve problems, achieve goals, and we find no real satisfaction in life without obstacles to conquer and goals to achieve. — Maxwell Maltz

In this chapter, I cover choosing your birth provider, address some facts to be aware of in regards to inductions and then look at all your options with a birth plan that you can tailor to your needs and wants.

Choosing your birth provider

Choosing your birth provider is a very important part of the process — getting this right is more important than people realise. Ensure you do your homework and research all the options available to you. This is not something you want to leave to chance. By doing so, you are taking an active role to ensure the best possible outcome for you, your partner and your soon-to-be-born baby. If you are birthing in a private hospital, check out their caesarian and intervention rates. A lot of the time they are higher than the public hospitals.

I had one woman who came to my birthing classes and as a result she realized she was unhappy with the private birthing facility she had booked. Their obstetrician had a high caesarean rate and for this, her first pregnancy, she wanted a natural birth. I recommended a home-birthing midwife and she had an amazing experience birthing at home. Proving it's never too late to change your plans.

It is important to work out what type of birthing day you want, and with the wide variety of choice that is now available to mothers, you will find what is perfect for you. Remember as well, that if you are not satisfied with the care you are receiving, say something. The birth of your child is an event that you will remember forever. Make sure your needs are being met, and if need be, give yourself permission to change.

I did make sure I affirmed that I would find the perfect place for me to birth my children. I knew I wanted a water birth if possible. I knew my preference was for a midwife led approach so I didn't see the need to pay for an obstetrician. All these values narrowed my search.

Midwife-run programs

Australia does have some excellent midwife-run programs and more recently, midwifery teams, so that the expectant couple get to know and birth with someone from their team, ideally creating continuity of care. You would have an opportunity to meet all of the midwives and feel confident that someone from your team will be at the birth. This means that, not only do you know them and have a greater sense of connection, they will also know you and your personal preferences.

Midwives have long been at the heart of women's birthing experiences, reaching far back into our collective history. They were called 'wise women' and in matriarchal societies, revered for their ability to bring life into the world until, in the appropriately named 'dark ages', the church shared the story of the curse of Eve. With the advent of the patriarchal society, many of the midwives at that time were burnt at the stake as witches, as their wisdom was seen as heretical. Along with this change came a very negative story of birth, from which we are still recovering.

Birth centres

Another excellent option is a birth centre. They are midwife-led and the focus is on natural birth. The rooms have a home-like feel to them and have much less of the medical equipment that you might find on a traditional labour ward. Some have baths for water births and they may have double beds for you and your partner to relax on. My husband really appreciated the double bed at 4 am, as did I! It can be very reassuring to be able to snuggle together in a comfortable way.

The birth centre is a great option if you are uncertain about a home birth and clear that you do want as natural a birth as possible. It can give you a sense of security. The birth centre does not offer epidurals however, it has the safety net of the hospital if life does throw you a curveball and you require assistance. It has a very noninvasive focus making it ideal for you if you want to experience a natural drug-free birth. They focus on natural comfort measures, they do still have gas, air and injections of pethidine or morphine if needed.

Home birth

In Australia, at the time of this writing, home births are a rare occurrence. It is an area of contention and seems to receive a lot of negative press. Having come from England where home birth is fully supported, I was quite amazed at the fear that home birth can cause. In the Netherlands, where home birth is around 30 per cent, research shows that planned home births where the mother has been assessed as low risk has favourable outcomes. The most obvious benefit for home birth is the comfort of being in your home surroundings. One of my doula clients was very comfortable while labouring at home and when it was time, lamented the need to go to hospital. A car journey while in labour does add another dimension to the process!

Should you decide to have a home birth, you will need to engage the services of an independent midwife. Having a baby isn't an illness, it is a normal natural function of the body. As long as it is an informed decision and you are having a low risk pregnancy, then home birth is a wonderful option. It is also one of the best ways to avoid interventionist obstetrics. Midwives are more than capable of delivering the best of care in the home environment. It also has the advantage that the birthing mother is not alone; either the midwife or the birthing partner is there the whole time to offer support. Home births are also not under the same time pressures as the labour ward, which can reduce some anxiety around the birth. There is also a sense of privacy that your home can offer which is not found in a hospital environment and all this adds to the peace and quiet that a home birth can offer. The midwife can even do all of the postnatal follow-up right in your home.

Obstetrician

In Australia it is quite common to engage the services of an obstetrician. Similar to buying a large ticket item, it is important to put in some time and energy into researching the best obstetrician for your needs. Having been brought up in England, I have experience in both the English and the Australian systems. Due to the National Health Service in England, the majority of the population goes through midwife led care. You would only see an obstetrician if there was a problem.

If you do decide that an obstetrician is the best course of action for you, please interview them. You are paying them after all. Ask important questions like: what is their rate of caesareans, inductions and episiotomies? Get a feel for their view of birth, does it match yours? There are wonderful mother-focused obstetricians to be found and on the other hand, there are some who are invested in interventionist obstetrics. They both have their place. Just ensure, if you do decide to have an obstetrician, that they are in step with you about the kind of birth you want. If you want a water birth, is that option available to you?

Inductions

In Australia, the rate of induction is around 25 percent. Many of those interventions could be reduced easily and safely. A lot of the problems we face during birth are a result of fear; not just the fear of birth, it is also the fear medical professionals have of being sued. The way the system works creates the increased likelihood of intervention as the medical profession is liable if they do not take action. As a consequence, we now have a culture of intervention. By taking responsibility for our choices, we take back our power and control. As long as you are making an informed decision and you are not taking any unnecessary risks, you can assert your needs with confidence. It is important to be clear in communicating what you want.

Most hospitals have a policy to induce labour at 40 weeks and the conversation to induce often begins around 38 weeks. That is earlier than the World Health Organization's definition of a prolonged gestation, which is 42+ weeks. Due dates have a lot to answer for as they have become the focus rather than letting the process unfold naturally in its own sweet time. Unfortunately, it looks like due dates are here to stay.

Approximately five percent of women give birth on their due date. 'Post-dates' means that you are past your given due date meaning: into your fortieth week. From this time, the medical world starts to focus on pathology — what can go wrong.

It is good to be aware that, according to the WHO, a baby is considered 'term' from 37 to 42 weeks. Yes, that's right, 42 weeks! The fear for the medical model is of the placenta breaking down. I learnt this the hard way for my first labour, and this hard-won lesson stood me in good stead subsequently, which I now pass onto you and to all my birthing ladies.

My experience

My first birth started with an induction. I was ten days over 40 weeks and the pressure was on me to go into labour. It was quite obvious however, when Lauren was born that she was not overdue, yet the seeds of fear had been sown for me to follow the path of induction.

With my second birth I had learnt the lessons from that induction. When I was nine days past my due date, induction was again brought up. I requested an ultrasound to check everything was as it should be; that there was no problem with my placenta or baby and that it was safe for me to wait to go into spontaneous labour. Which I did do — on day 10! There is a marked difference in a labour that is forced to start versus a natural spontaneous labour. While I was still lucky enough to have a vaginal delivery with the induction, it was a much more intense process, as well as having to experience the discomfort of the delightfully named 'strip and stretch!', Prostaglandin gel inserted vaginally and the breaking of my waters — not my most fun day!

The statistics show a steep rise of inductions in recent years. A study of 1.5 million births found that there has been a shift towards inducing labour which cannot be explained by medical need (Amy Corderoy, *Sydney Morning Herald*, 16 July 2011). With this rise, studies have shown there has also been a rise in caesareans, regardless of the fact that the overall number of women actually requesting a caesarean is low. Between 2001 and 2007 only 44.9 percent of women who had an induction went on to have a vaginal birth—that's less than half!

With those odds in mind, ensure you get all the facts before you agree to an induction. Always ask why they are suggesting it. Make sure you are happy with the reason and remember that you can explore other options. It is your body and you hold all the power, so ensure you make an informed decision that is right for you.

What does an induction entail?

An induction can start with a 'strip and stretch' also known as 'sweeping the membranes'. The theory here is to irritate your cervix so that it will release natural prostaglandins to soften or ripen the cervix ready for labour. If this doesn't start your labour, artificial prostaglandins are then inserted vaginally next to the cervix in the form of a gel, sticky tape or pessary. This will be absorbed locally and can kick-start your labour. It can also soften and open your cervix enough for another procedure, an amniotomy or the breaking of your waters, to be performed. This is where an 'amnihook' (which looks like a long crochet needle) is inserted vaginally to hook and burst the membranes. This is followed by the sensation of the warm water, or 'liquor' as it is known, running down your legs, which feels like you have wet yourself! This can bring you into labour spontaneously, which was my experience, or you may wait a few hours to see if labour starts.

If you need further intervention, the next phase is an IV drip of artificial oxytocin (Pitocin or Syntocinon) usually administered into the vein on the back of your hand. These stimulate your uterus to contract and can be a lot more intense than naturally occurring contractions. The pattern and intensity builds more quickly than a typical spontaneous labour. The synthetic oxytocin doesn't cross the blood-brain barrier in the same way naturally occurring oxytocin does in labour, therefore you miss out on the feel-good endorphins that oxytocin normally produces.

You will also be continuously monitored, which can restrict your movement. Following your baby's birth, you may still require the drip of oxytocin to deliver the placenta, as you may not be producing enough oxytocin on your own. On the other hand, you can feel confident Mother Nature has provided you with all you need to have a natural third stage.

By agreeing to an induction, there is the understanding that either you, or your baby, is currently at risk. In this medical model, you will be classed as high-risk and that an expedient delivery is the best option. Once you have started down the path of having an induction you must be prepared for having all of the interventions of induction. It becomes a domino effect, from one intervention to the next. Hopefully you can see how your chance of a vaginal birth may decrease if you are induced before you are naturally ready.

It is important to remember that there are natural methods of induction that you can explore first: acupuncture, reflexology, homeopathy, and chiropractic treatments. Of course, we must not forget nipple stimulation and sex, as both produce oxytocin and semen contains prostaglandins!

If you do need to have an induction for medical reasons, your preparation to keep you relaxed, calm and focused on the result you want will be even more important. It can greatly increase your chances of a vaginal delivery which can still be done, as I did with Lauren.

Your birth plan

Predict another good day for yourself, expect something good to happen. — Mack Douglass

It is a good idea to plan ahead for something as important as the birth of your baby, just like the emergency briefing on an aeroplane prior to take-off. This is where a birth plan comes in. Remember, the emergency briefing is not a prediction; if you do find yourself in an unexpected situation, your birth plan ensures you have already thought about it and can then make an informed decision and everyone can be clear on what is needed. (See the birth plan template below.)

Being prepared will make things easier for you and will prevent feelings of regret because life 'threw you a curveball' and you didn't know how best to respond. Preparation also creates confidence as you gain a greater understanding of just what is involved and how you can take charge of your birthing experience.

Make sure you, your birthing partner and your healthcare providers have discussed all the options fully so you can have a plan for any situation. Remember that you are always free to change your mind. Your birth plan is a guide for your birthing intention; it is not set in stone.

In the birth plan we will look at who you would like to have present during your birthing, the kind of atmosphere you want to create, how you want to make the process comfortable for you, what positions and what props you may wish to use to aid your comfort and relaxation.

The plan covers what options are available should you require some help, including pain management and caesarean.

MY BIRTH INTENTIONS

NAME: _____

INDUCTION

If baby and I are well, I would like my baby to decide his/her own due date.

I am happy to discuss a plan should my pregnancy reach the end of term at 42 weeks.

If labour induction seems a possibility, my preference is to explore all natural means first. Such as: acupuncture, chiropractor, massage, reflexology, nipple stimulation and/or additional physical intimacy with my partner to release oxytocin.

Thank you.

I would like the following people to be present during labour and/or birth:

Partner: _____
Friend/s: _____
Relative/s: _____
Doula: _____

I would like to:

- ☐ Bring music
- ☐ Dim the lights
- ☐ Wear my own clothes during labour and delivery
- ☐ Take pictures and/or video during labour and delivery

ON ADMISSION AND BIRTHING

Please refrain from asking me if I am in pain or offering pain medication, as I am aware of the options for pain relief and will ask if I feel I require anything.

I would like:

- ☐ The option of returning home if I'm less than 4 cm dilated
- ☐ My partner to be allowed to stay with me at all times

Gentle Birthing

- ☐ To be asked permission should a student wish to observe
- ☐ To eat during labour should I feel hungry
- ☐ To stay hydrated by drinking clear fluids
- ☐ To walk, move around and use birthing equipment as I choose
- ☐ Minimal vaginal examinations

LABOUR PROPS

If available, please can I use:

☐ Birthing stool	☐ Birthing pool/tub	☐ Shower
☐ Birthing ball	☐ Squatting bar	☐ Heat/cold pack

TO MAINTAIN MY COMFORT

I would like to use the following techniques:

- ☐ Self-hypnosis
- ☐ Breathing
- ☐ Bath/shower
- ☐ Massage
- ☐ Hot/cold packs
- ☐ Acupressure
- ☐ Homeopathic remedies
- ☐ Changing birthing positions
- ☐ Other: _____

To affirm, please refrain from offering pain medication. I will request it if I need it.

If I decide I want medical pain relief, I would prefer:

- ☐ Systemic medication: paracetamol, water injection, panadeine forte, opiate injection
- ☐ Regional analgesia (an epidural and/or spinal block)

NATURAL BIRTH

During delivery, I please request:

- □ The room to be as quiet as possible
- □ To allow me to choose to gently breathe my baby down
- □ Be allowed to progress free of time limits as long as my baby and I are doing well
- □ View my baby crowning using a mirror
- □ Touch my baby's head as it crowns
- □ Have an episiotomy only if medically required
- □ Time allowed for the perineum to stretch naturally
- □ To birth into water
- □ To hold my baby right away, delay any unnecessary procedures
- □ Other _____

I'd like to try the following positions for pushing (and birth):

- □ Semi-reclining
- □ Side-lying position
- □ Squatting
- □ Hands and knees
- □ Whatever feels right at the time

After birth, I please request:

- □ To wait until the umbilical cord stops pulsating before it's clamped and cut
- □ For my partner to cut the umbilical cord
- □ To breastfeed as soon as possible
- □ To have a natural third stage of delivery, i.e. time allowed for this process
- □ To have a managed third stage of delivery
- □ A Lotus Birth
- □ Vitamin K oral doses
- □ or Vitamin K injection

CORD BLOOD BANKING

I'm planning to:

- ☐ Donate cord blood to a public bank
- ☐ Bank cord blood privately
- ☐ None of the above

C-SECTION

If I require a C-section, I please request:

- ☐ My partner is present during the operation
- ☐ The screen lowered a bit so I can see my baby being delivered
- ☐ The baby is given to me or my partner as soon as appropriate
- ☐ To breastfeed my baby in the recovery room
- ☐ The baby to stay with my partner and/or myself

OTHER INTERVENTIONS

As long as the baby and I are doing well, I'd like to be allowed to progress free of time limits and have my labour augmented only when necessary.

Thank you for honouring our requests and we understand that these choices may change in light of special circumstances. We are very grateful for your care and support in the birth of our baby.

In summary:

- The decision you make in choosing your provider and place of birth has a massive impact on the outcome so ensure you do your homework.
- Make a list of your priorities as this will give you clarity, help you narrow your search, and help you find your perfect place.
- If you choose to birth in a private hospital, check out their caesarian and intervention rates; frequently the rates are higher than public hospitals.
- If you are being offered an induction, please ensure that you have a sound reason for the procedure. Exercise all the natural options and be proactive in creating the birth you want.
- Ensure you have discussed and are clear about your birth plan, so that if life does throw a curveball, you are aware of how to make the best of the situation.
- Understanding, and being prepared for any of the possible circumstances, allows you to have the confidence to make the best possible choice for the best possible outcome, regardless of the situation.

Chapter 7:
Harnessing the power of hypnosis and affirmations

Language is the oxygen of thinking; it allows thoughts to breathe and live, to be full-bodied. — Caterina Rando

In this chapter, we will explore hypnosis and its benefits.

Hypnosis

Hypnosis is used in such a diverse variety of areas, from entertainment on TV and in live shows to sports, psychology and the medical world. There are many varied points of views and differing techniques.

My preferred definition of hypnosis is from the textbook *Trancework* by Michael D. Yapko, which is used for teaching hypnosis: "It is a focused experience of attentional absorption that invites people to respond experientially on multiple levels to amplify and utilize their personal resources."

For me, the most important aspect of hypnosis is the focus and absorption of attention. Even if you have never experienced formal clinical hypnosis in a therapeutic setting, you will have still experienced a similar focus and absorption of your attention. For example, think about when you first learnt to drive; it was a very conscious activity where you needed to pay close attention to everything. Yet, once you reached a certain level of competency with driving, it became second nature. Your focus and attention would have shifted from the mechanics of physically driving to it becoming a more unconscious action where your mind can wander. I'm sure you have had the experience of the hypnotic effect of motorway driving where the road races monotonously by and you arrive at your destination not remembering a lot or parts of the journey!

Another example of a hypnotic state is going to the movies. I love going to the movies, especially to see some of the 3D adventure movies out nowadays, as my focus and attention is fully absorbed. I get lost in the characters and story and transport mentally to different times, places or worlds. I still know I am in a movie theatre and yet my focus is fully absorbed in what I see up on the screen.

Likewise, my husband always jokes that he can't be hypnotised, yet sometimes when I speak to him, I know he is in a trance and I get no response! I'm sure we've all had that experience when someone has been talking to us, and we haven't been present. This is when our attention has been focused and absorbed inwardly.

The other important aspect of hypnosis is tapping into a person's own personal resources. I have watched some women who may, in their other world run their own company or have high-powered corporate jobs, seem to forget all of their many strengths that can transfer into the birthing arena. We all have gifts and talents that we have acquired over the years. I love the way that their abilities can be highlighted and utilised using hypnosis during the birthing, eliminating all fixed ideas of lack and returning to their innate resilience.

The benefits of hypnosis

It is now understood that during pregnancy and prior to birth, the use of hypnosis can significantly shorten labour, reduce pain and reduce the need for intervention. Practitioners also understand that mothers who used hypnosis to relax and calm themselves during pregnancy and birth, have babies who are much more likely to sleep and feed better.

Hypnosis is an experiential process and can assist you in time distortion. This can be useful especially in allowing you to perceive your contractions as shorter periods of time and the time between contractions as a longer period of time. Hypnosis can also increase responsiveness to suggestion so that fears can be addressed, released and reframed.

A lot of the current problems we face with birth can be viewed as being the result of mass hypnosis working negatively. Many people buy into the current view that birth is a problematic event to be endured, and that their bodies are destined to fail and that they will require painful medical intervention.

This form of hypnosis is all too common and ends up being proven right; what the thinker thinks, the prover proves. As a result of this, mothers are going into their birth experience full of fear and tension, which in turn increases their experience of pain due to the physiological response to stress and anxiety in the body.

Unfortunately, hypnosis has negative connotations for a lot of people, which is such a shame as it has the potential to assist many birthing mums.

My experience with hypnosis

From my own personal experience, hypnosis was a fantastic tool during my pregnancy to assist me in relaxing, to help focus my mind on how I wanted to experience labour and enable me in feeling confident about the inevitable process. Instead I was excited about this amazing rite of passage and avoided all the fear, along with all the possible problems that being fearful could bring into my birthing process.

I was fortunate to train with Michael Yapko, who has been working in the field of hypnosis and clinical psychology for over 40 years. With a solid knowledge base and vast experience, Yapko is an amazing teacher. I was lucky enough to have a session of hypnosis with him when my name was pulled out of the hat after I attended his keynote. (Previously, I met him while on the board of the Australian Society of Clinical Hypnotherapists when he was a keynote speaker at their 2010 conference.)

After seeing one of his clinical videos of hypnosis, which he showed at the 2010 conference, I was amazed at what he was able to achieve in 27 minutes! His workshop was at the start of school holidays and having two school-age children, I had decided not to go. After seeing him deliver his keynote, I asked him what the workshop entailed. He told me that it would be a lot more experiential learning, and we would get to practice what he was teaching. He then mentioned that he also has a practical demonstration on stage, attendees can put their name in a hat and that a name is picked out to have a session to work on a problem area in their life on stage with him. At that point I heard my internal voice say very calmly to me 'that's going to be me' to which I thought to myself incredulously 'but I'm not even going to the workshop!'. I told Janine, a friend of mine, who was also on the board and very much an intuitive person and she said that maybe I should rethink my decision.

I got solution focused and managed to find a friend willing and able to take care of my two children for the required days and convinced my long-suffering husband that $600 for the workshop was a great investment — and it was!

Having my name picked out of the hat blew me away, especially since I nearly didn't put my name in as I didn't know what I would work on. Janine however, pushed me saying 'do it about your work'. Thank you, Janine!

The subsequent session was amazing. I was able to get first-hand experience of Yapko's style of hypnosis, which is very different from the more authoritarian style that I had been taught and had previously experienced. He also used the skills I already possessed, along with metaphors, or stories, to highlight possible solutions. After the session, I felt ecstatic. He was able to help me shift the limitations of my point of view by highlighting the missing piece in my knowledge and show me the necessary skills required to complete the jigsaw. I also got a valuable lesson in trusting my intuition, the wisdom of my deeper self. While Yapko is a science-based man (which is great and I respect his point of view), I have the additional perspective: I know I am divinely guided by wisdom.

When Yapko came to Sydney to teach a 100 Hour Hypnosis Training program in 2013, I was there to learn more. He did not disappoint. In fact, I still listen to that original recorded session. I know that it has helped me to continue to move forward in the direction of my calling — to help women and their partners to birth in a calm, relaxed state of love and joy rather than fear and pain.

Hypnosis as a tool for birthing

I feel there has never been a better time for birthing couples to explore the power of their mind, using hypnosis as a tool, to focus on how they wish to experience their birth. Using hypnosis for the birth of both my children certainly gave me the confidence to have a drug-free birth, and like most pregnant women, I did have a certain amount of trepidation about the whole thing!

In his books, Yapko reminds us that responsiveness to hypnosis should not be confused with being gullible, as you are always able to reject suggestions that are not desirable or relevant for you. It is important that you find a clinical hypnotherapist with whom you feel comfortable and has your best interests in mind, as this will enhance your responsiveness and ultimately your result.

The 'Hypnosis Antenatal Training for Childbirth (HATCh): a Randomised Controlled Trial' See https://bmcpregnancychildbirth.biomedcentral.com/ articles/10.1186/1471-2393-6-5. The trial concluded that those women along with their partner who attended antenatal education classes with hypnosis and breathing techniques were given a powerful and useful intervention, and partners were given the confidence to challenge professionals in order to achieve the mothers' desired outcomes.

Creative visualisation

To my mind, there is a lot of similarity between hypnosis, creative visualisation and guided meditation. They just come from different parts of the world — hypnosis and creative visualisation from the West and meditation from the East — but ultimately they all can create the same results.

Guided meditation is a form of meditation where an individual is guided into a relaxed state of consciousness either by someone in person or by a recording of a voice. Creative visualisation is the technique of using your imagination to make something you want, happen. By directing positive energy and envisioning what you want your life to be, you can make that vision a reality.

Creative visualisation takes discipline. A lot of the time we are visualising in the wrong direction; focusing on what we *don't* want. The general images we have of birth are what we see in television and films, and often we replay these scenesmentally, to our cultural detriment.

It is important when using creative visualisation that you use all of your senses as this will give you the complete picture. As well as visualising your ideal birth, expand your focus to incorporate what it will feel like to experience your baby in your arms after an amazingly relaxed birth. Feel the joy and imagine the voice of the midwife as she congratulates you on such a perfect birth. What thoughts are you having?

With creative visualisation, it is important to have a belief that what you are visualising will happen, just as John F. Kennedy strongly believed that they could put a man on the moon. In comparison, natural birth is far easier! After all, it has been done many times and will continue to be done many times in the future. It is your birthing ability that you need to have certainty in. I know you can do it!

Working with affirmations and afformations

Affirmations are a great way to declare your intention. These are statements that affirm or, 'declare positively', and are termed in the present tense. For example, 'I have an easy, smooth birth', or 'I have the perfect midwife for the birth of my baby'. Only you can decide what wording will work best for you.

When choosing affirmations in regard to birthing, notice if you have any negative thoughts or fears about your birth, then use an affirmation as the antidote. This ensures that you are using your thoughts to focus on what you do want.

Our thoughts have an impact on our feelings and also on the vibration that we send out into the world. Certain thoughts can become habitual and focusing on something different can sometimes feel forced. If you can hear yourself answering back an opposing thought that your new thought won't work, or isn't true, phrase it as a question. 'Afformations', a phrase coined by Noah St. John, are just that, asking an empowering question. This approach allows your powerful mind to search for the answer to your question. For example, 'What makes it so easy to stay relaxed during my birth?' 'What allows me to have the best support during my birth?' and so on.

As well as sending out a certain vibration, our thoughts impact our mood or state of mind and can change the way we behave, which in turn affects our results. For instance, if I constantly think I won't be able to cope with the birth of my baby, not only will this thought lower my vibration, it will also leave me feeling hopeless and helpless. This, in turn, will create anxiety as I project a negative outcome into my future. Given my brain doesn't recognise the difference between an actual or an imaginary perceived threat, it responds by flooding my system with adrenaline as the fight-or-flight response kicks in and I tense up. All of this contributes to creating pain in my body and I end up creating what I feared: that I couldn't cope with the birth of my baby. This then reinforces my initial thought and the cycle perpetuates.

Fortunately, affirmations or afformations also work in the other direction. For instance, by stating 'I have an easy, smooth, natural birth and I am powerful' you will in turn relax as you project what you want into your future. Endorphins (a neurotransmitter) are then released, which bond to pain receptor sites and assist in creating comfort and further relaxation. This then reinforces your affirmation and you are on a roll. Once you start to think in an affirming way it leads to the next positive thought.

Thoughts + Actions = Results

When you impress an idea onto your subconscious mind, it alters the vibration of the instrument that we know as 'our body'. Meditation is one way to listen to your stream of thoughts, observe them and not to get attached to them. Again, it is important that you don't judge your thoughts as this can affect your feelings and lower your vibration, especially if they are self-deprecating. Therefore, notice and don't resist any negative thoughts, just be mindful. By noticing negative thoughts, you can begin to let go of attachment to them after all, it is just a thought. Awareness is where it starts.

Remember, the old saying 'what you resist persists'. Another way of looking at it is that as the observer of your thoughts you can just notice them. For example: "there's that thought about labouring for days and being so exhausted again. Oh well, it doesn't mean anything." That way you are detaching from the meaning of the thought, so it will have no charge to it and be neutral. It is very important to understand that just because you think something doesn't mean that it is true. If you have a negative thought you can choose not to attach any meaning to it.

Play with looking at your thoughts and choosing wonderful, empowering afformations or affirmations. Make them a kind of mantra, especially if someone decides to tell you a birth horror story. Remind yourself that whatever they are saying, it doesn't mean it will happen to you. Instead, refocus on what you want to happen.

In summary:

- Create time in your day to focus your mind, relax and go within to visualise your ideal birth.
- Remember to incorporate feeling positive emotions and the use of all of your senses to create a complete visualisation.
- Practice meditation. Start with a couple of minutes if you have not practiced it before and build up your time.
- Notice how your thoughts impact your actions and can therefore determine your results and reinforce your original thought. I like the way Sydney Banks, a theosophist, spoke of thoughts being like a rudder of a ship. They can take you to crash on the rocks or out to calm waters.

- Think and speak positively about how your birth experience will be.
- Remember: You have free will to choose the thoughts you focus on, so exercise your mental muscles and aim for calm!
- Your feelings are a guidance system informing you of the quality of your current thoughts. If you are feeling anxious, angry or upset, these feelings are telling you that your thinking is off course and you are always free to think differently.

Chapter 8:
Disappearing fear and its effects

Be afraid of nothing - you have within you all wisdom, all power, all strength, all understanding. — Eileen Caddy.

An excellent way to let go and get rid of unwanted subconscious programs, or as Joe Vitale, author and spiritual teacher termed it, 'counter intentions', is with the use of the Emotional Freedom Technique (EFT). This simple process is very powerful, primarily because it can change your brain!

Fear and the body's stress response

The stress response, which activates and creates a chemical response in your body, is first triggered in the midbrain, sometimes referred to as the limbic system. The amygdala, a component of the limbic system, is the source of your long-term memory and emotions and is also where negative experiences are encoded. The role of the amygdala is to alert us to a possible threat to our survival and trigger the fight-or-flight response. While this has obvious benefits, it can also cause problems. In the case of pregnancy and birth, going to a hospital and seeing technical equipment may create anxiety, especially if your previous experiences of hospitals have been problematic. Once our amygdala has alerted us to a possible threat, our body chemistry is then activated, and we are at the mercy of our subconscious programs and contaminated thinking.

As mentioned in earlier chapters, there are so many negative stories and perceptions around birth that it is no wonder that fear, pain and tension are the typical pathway in many births. Yet with advances in science, the evidence is now proving what Grantly Dick Read, an obstetrician from the 1900s, realised over 70 years ago. Fear, whether perceived or actual, sets up a physiological response that hampers the birthing process.

How can EFT resolve this potential reaction?

Research has shown that stimulating certain acupressure points on select meridian lines resulted in decreased activity in the amygdala, and other parts of the brain associated with fear. MRI scans of the brain during this process show the amygdala's alert response being switched off. As a result, EFT (sometimes also referred to as 'tapping') can be used effectively to remove fears pregnant women may have about their labour and birth, such as not being able to cope with the birth of their baby, anxieties about changes to their life after the birth, or becoming a parent and/or adding to their family dynamics.

I recommend you read Nick Ortner's *The Tapping Solution* or watch his documentary of the same name. It really is inspiring. I have personally experienced the benefits of EFT. I have also helped others to break free of their fears and limiting beliefs using this technique. It may seem a little strange at first — it did for me when I first tried it eight years ago now — and yet the results and shifts in how I felt kept me curious and willing to learn more about it. One of the great things about EFT is that it is so simple to learn, anyone can use it. EFT has many applications but in this chapter I focus on using it to deal with fears and anxieties around birth.

How do you 'tap'?

The procedure of tapping consists of rating the emotional intensity of your reaction to a specific issue, on a scale of 1 to 10 and then repeating an orienting affirmation (a 'setup statement') while tapping specific points on the body. Your emotional intensity is then re-scored and the process repeated (if necessary) until you have little or no emotional intensity (0-2 on the scale).

To practice, let's focus on limiting thoughts or fears about your upcoming birthing. Score yourself on a scale of 0 to 10 on how anxious or scared you might be about giving birth — 10 representing that you are feeling highly anxious and 0 meaning all is well. Make a note of this score so you can monitor your progress and see how things change for you.

After you have recorded your initial score, you need to create a 'setup statement' using the traditional EFT phrase: 'Even though I am _____, I totally love and accept myself.' You then need to fill the blank area in with a brief description of the negative emotion or problem you want to address.

An example setup statement might be:

- 'Even though I am feeling anxious about giving birth to my baby, I totally love and accept myself.'
- 'Even though I am scared I might not be able to handle giving birth to my baby, I totally love and accept myself.'
- 'Even though I am worried about giving birth, I totally love and accept myself.'

Commence tapping by saying your setup statement three times while using the fingertips of one hand on the karate chopping side on your other hand.

Figure 8.1: Say your setup statement three times while using the fingertips of one hand on the karate chopping side on your other hand

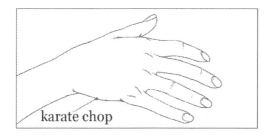

karate chop

Using your fingertips, tap seven times on each of the following eight points in the EFT sequence while voicing your statements:

1. Eyebrow
2. Side of eye
3. Under eye
4. Under nose
5. Under bottom lip
6. Collar bone
7. Underarm
8. Top of head

Figure 8.2: The eight points of the EFT sequence

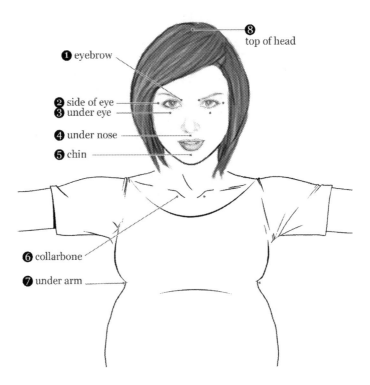

While you are tapping, allow any thoughts, fears and anxieties that arise from giving birth flow through.

Note: It is important to tap on the negatives, which is often shunned. The self-help approach does drum into us the importance of focusing on the positive; while this is important, it is essential to acknowledge the negative as it may be a counter-intention to our conscious mind's desires, thereby creating sabotage or unwanted circumstances. Without clearing the negative, those thoughts can potentially trigger the amygdala and the survival fight or flight response, possibly hampering your birthing process.

In his book, Nick Ortner cleverly observes the negative thoughts we tap on as the 'truth' because this is what is really hiding under our positive affirmations. Once we have acknowledged and released this 'truth', the way is cleared and we can then tap into the way nature intended — the inspirational, the ideal and the empowering, real truth.

Here are some suggested groups of phrases for each of the points (as indicated by the numbering). These are based on the typical fears and anxieties I have heard about birth from couples over the many years I have been teaching. Rest assured, there is no wrong way to do this, so please tap on any fears that you may have or that come to your mind while tapping.

1. This fear I am feeling.
2. I am worried that I will not cope during the birth.
3. What if it is all too much?
4. I am scared I might tear badly in the process.
5. This fear I am feeling is that my body might fail me.
6. I am scared that I might do lots of hard work and then need a caesarean.
7. I am scared I won't be able to handle it.
8. I feel fearful that everything may go wrong.

1. I am scared for my baby's safety.
2. I don't like needles.
3. I feel fearful of having an epidural.
4. I am scared of medical intervention.
5. I am fearful of extended and exhausting labour.
6. I feel overwhelmed.
7. What if I can't relax?
8. I am scared my body may never be the same again.

Gentle Birthing

1. So much confusion.
2. So much anxiety.
3. Feeling scared.
4. So much worry.
5. This fear around giving birth.
6. This fear around becoming a parent.
7. So much fear.
8. Releasing all this fear around birth.

1. I relax about the birth now.
2. I trust my body's innate ability to birth.
3. Birth is safe.
4. I am safe.
5. My baby is safe.
6. My body knows exactly what to do.
7. I relax about giving birth.
8. I trust the process.

1. I attract all the right circumstances to create my ideal birth.
2. All is well.
3. I am safe.
4. I relax my mind and body now.
5. I feel calm and peaceful about birth and parenting.
6. Trusting the process.
7. I intuitively know how to birth.
8. Deeply relaxed.

Finish the process with a deep breath in and a deep breath out.

Having completed your round of tapping, notice how you feel regarding the initial issue raised. Rate yourself again on a scale of 0 to 10; with a 0 meaning you don't feel any stress and 10 is the most distress you can imagine. Hopefully after the tapping your score will have come down considerably. If you need to reduce it further, you can complete a tapping sequence again.

As mentioned, the above phrases are just suggestions. You may find that you have other fears that jump into your mind while you are tapping. If so, use them; acknowledge what is your truth at this point without judgement.

Work through the fear points in order, until you feel ready to tap on how you want it to be, the expanded truth.

In the case of birthing, often the root of a problem to be tapped on is a limiting belief that you may have or that society generally has about birthing. Getting free of limiting beliefs and replacing them with empowering truths about your innate abilities, strengths and potential, as well as nature's amazing biological mechanisms will create positive energy within your system. Limitations can weigh heavily on your mind and within your energetic fields, whereas the truth is liberating and feels light.

In summary:

- The amygdala in your brain fires off when it perceives a possible threat or danger, both real or imagined.
- By acknowledging your fears while tapping on certain acupressure points, this response can be shut down and you can return to your natural state of calm.
- Once fears are acknowledged, you can then overlay them with an expanded truth of how you want to experience things.

Conclusion:
A little reminder

Birth is a physical, emotional and spiritual journey, and even though the distance the baby has to travel is not far, it is best for you to be well prepared for the process. The best state you can choose to be is optimistic, relaxed and excited about this most beautiful, transformational and expansive miracle. This applies not only to birthing but life in general.

I hope that you get to see, as I did, that your thoughts are creative. They can inspire you to imagine and create consciously what you desire, when infused with love and joy. Life is not meant to be difficult and yet our thinking can make it so! Daydream about your ideal, relaxed, comfortable and joyous birthing and imagine how you want it to be.

Ask for divine guidance, for the ideal circumstances and keep your unwavering focus on the result you wish to experience. Trust and believe in your ability to birth with ease, and ignore the naysayers as well as those who want to tell you of birthing horror stories — your experience is yours to create.

Remember that the four-minute mile was once considered beyond human capabilities, yet Roger Banister was convinced otherwise. Once he had broken this limiting belief, others soon followed. Now even high school students can attain this feat, once considered impossible! As more women experience and talk about their smooth, natural and gentle birthing, the ripple effect will be banishing fear. This approach will have a positive impact on others' births by creating ripples of change and will soon become the norm. This is how a shift in paradigm happens — after all, everyone once believed that the world was flat!

Easy, empowering births are yours to claim as of right now! If I, and many others can do it, so can you. Be inspired by others who have walked this path successfully before you, trust their stories and release any doubts and fears. As Franklin Roosevelt said, "You have nothing to fear except fear itself." Birth is an amazing process, a short distance for the baby to travel and immense transformation for all involved. It will be remembered by you, your partner and your baby too.

Using the tools and knowledge you have gained from this book I invite you to take charge of your birthing experience. Remember that you hold the power and you are responsible for your choices. Visualisation, education, relaxation and focusing on how you are going to experience birth will help you create your reality, along with a healthcare provider who honours your choices.

Birth does not need to be a medical event; you have innate birthing abilities that just require the right environment, understanding and trust.

It is time for women and their partners to take back birthing, one baby at a time and it is my sincere wish that this book gives you the tools to create your ideal, natural, gentle birthing. To bring birth out of fear and pain and back into joy and love, as nature intended. It is well within your capabilities and has the potential to assist you in realising your power, strength and resilience, which are great assets on the next step of your journey as a parent.

Life is best played as a 'go for it' process, so aim high, focus on how wonderful the birth will be, remember that you are the writer, director and star of your movie. Just take the steps as laid out for you in this book and you can create your success because life loves you and supports you.

Printed in the United States
By Bookmasters